Daughter
of
Atholl

Lady Evelyn Stewart Murray
1868–1940

SYLVIA ROBERTSON AND PATRICIA YOUNG

ABERTAY
HISTORICAL
SOCIETY

NUMBER 36
DUNDEE
1997

Lady Evelyn Stewart Murray in her garden in Spa, Belgium 1920. Taken by her brother Lord James, who wrote: 'I have been endeavouring to photograph her unawares – I managed to get two indifferent snapshots while she thought I was taking the house – Her suspicions are now aroused however and she flies whenever she sees the Camera.' This is one of only two photographs of Evelyn taken after 1914. (KM82 and Duke of Atholl's Collection)

ACKNOWLEDGEMENTS

Our grateful thanks go to the many people who have helped the preparation of this book, but in particular we wish to record our appreciation and offer our sincere thanks to the following people and organisations:

In Scotland: His Grace, the 10th Duke of Atholl, for allowing us to use the Atholl Archives at Blair Castle; Mrs Jane Anderson, Archivist at Blair Castle, for her patience, unfailing help and encouragement; Mrs Ryder, Senior Guide, Blair Castle; Mr Christopher Davey and Dr Christopher Whatley, Abertay Historical Society, for their support and advice; Dr Alan Bruford, Archivist in the School of Scottish Studies, Edinburgh; Miss Helen Jackson and Roger Leitch, for their helpful comments and suggestions; Mrs Gill Forsyth, who typeset the Atholl Family tree; Staff of the Scottish National Library and Royal College of Physicians Library in Edinburgh and the Sandeman Library in Perth; Anna-Lise Robertson, translator, Pitlochry; Jim Duguid and Phil Forsyth.

In England: Mrs Elizabeth Elvin, Royal School of Needlework; Miss Santina Levey, formerly Keeper of the Department of Textiles and Dress, Victoria and Albert Museum, London; Dr Irvine Loudon, research associate, the Wellcome Unit for the History of Medicine in the University of Oxford; Miss Kim Reynolds, research assistant, New Dictionary of National Biography, Oxford; Royal Pharmaceutical Society of Great Britain; Schering Health Care.

In Switzerland: Madame Luthi-Graf, Historienne et Archiviste, Commune de Montreux.

In Belgium: Musée Royal d'Art et d'Histoire, Brussels; Mr L. Zylbergeld, Archiviste-Conservateur, Musées Communaux, Brussels; Mr Nigel Park, St Andrew's Church of Scotland, Brussels; Mr H. Installe, Archiviste de la ville de Malines; Mr Marcel Kocken, Malines; Mr Jean Toussaint, Bibliothécaire principal, Bibliothèque Communale de Spa; Dr Henrard, President du Conseil d'Administration du Musée de Spa.

We would like to record our special thanks to Brooking, Duncan and Seonag, who have had to share their homes with Evelyn for a number of years, and have done so with remarkable tolerance and patience.

CONTENTS

LIST OF ILLUSTRATIONS

ABBREVIATIONS

Atholl Archives	Atholl Archives in Blair Castle (SRO NRA 234 and 930)
SRO	Scottish Record Office
ESM	Lady Evelyn Stewart Murray
7th D of A	John, 7th Duke of Atholl
Duch L	Louisa, Duchess of Atholl
M of T	John George, Marquis of Tullibardine
8th D of A	John, 8th Duke of Atholl
March of T	Katharine, Marchioness of Tullibardine
Duch K	Katharine, Duchess of Atholl
JSM	Lord James Stewart Murray
9th D of A	James, 9th Duke of Atholl
Dow D of A	Anne, Dowager Duchess of Atholl
E MacG	Miss Emily Murray MacGregor

John George, Marquis of Tullibardine, succeeded his father as 8th Duke of Atholl in January 1917, at which date his wife, Katharine, Marchioness of Tullibardine, became Duchess of Atholl.

Lord James Stewart Murray succeeded his brother as 9th Duke of Atholl in March 1942.

```
                                                          John, 3rd D
                                                               1729

        ┌───────────────────────────────────────────────────────────
   John, 4th Duke of Atholl = Jane Cathcart
        1755-1830          │   1754-1790
              ┌────────────────────────────────────────────┐
       John, 5th Duke of Atholl                    Lord James Murray
            1778-1846                                   1782-1837
                  ┌──────────────────────────────────────────
   George, 6th Duke of Atholl = Anne Home Drummond
        1814-1864            │   1814-1897
                  ┌──────────┘
   John, 7th Duke of Atholl = Louisa Moncreiffe
        1840-1917              1844-1902
 ┌────────────────────────────────────┬───────────────────────────
Lady Dorothea = Harold Ruggles-Brise   Lady Helen = David Tod    Lady Ev
  (Dertha)         1864-1927           1867-1934   1859-1933     1868-1
 1866-1937
```

George Ia

Based on the family tree in "The
                                  compiled

OLL FAMILY

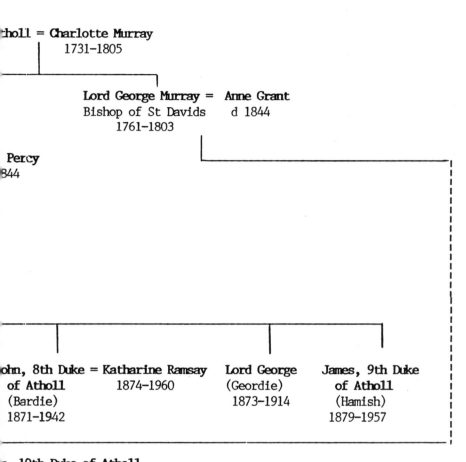

:holl = Charlotte Murray
       1731-1805

Lord George Murray = Anne Grant
Bishop of St Davids   d 1844
     1761-1803

Percy
844

ohn, 8th Duke = Katharine Ramsay   Lord George   James, 9th Duke
  of Atholl   1874-1960   (Geordie)   of Atholl
  (Bardie)   1873-1914   (Hamish)
  1871-1942   1879-1957

y, 10th Duke of Atholl
931-1996

les of the Atholl and Tullibardine Families"
, 7th Duke of Atholl

CHAPTER 1

Introduction

Lady Evelyn Stewart Murray (1868–1940) was a woman out of step. The youngest daughter of the 7th Duke of Atholl, she had the privileged upbringing of a member of the most aristocratic family in Highland Perthshire. Like most women of her class in the Victorian era, her education was elitist and geared towards the social graces, with the ultimate aim of finding her a suitable husband. But Evelyn committed the sin of refusing to conform. An intelligent, but also highly strung young woman, she was not satisfied by the seasonal round of social events and turned to more intellectual pursuits.

The Stewarts, from whom the present line is descended, were given the lands of Atholl in 1457[1] and over the years they acquired more land, wealth and power. By Evelyn's time the family had lost much of its former political influence. However, the estate still had 160 farms and extended from Dalnacardoch to Dunkeld, Strathardle to Strath Tay, a total of approximately 350,000 acres, mainly moorland and mountain. The estate provided work for a large number of people, including farmers, foresters, keepers and hillmen, as well as domestic staff who served the Duke and his family at Blair Castle and the Duke's mother, the Dowager Duchess Anne, at her home in Dunkeld. While the Duke and his mother clearly felt it their duty to do all they could to help their employees, both maintained a strict feudal attitude towards them, with Evelyn's mother, Duchess Louisa, being especially conscious of her social standing.

A number of women in the Atholl family have, over the centuries, achieved a great deal. Notable examples are Katharine Hamilton,[2] first wife of the 1st Duke, who had some political influence in the early eighteenth century; Lady Charlotte,[3] daughter of the 3rd Duke, who was a keen botanist and author of *The British Garden* in 1799; Anne Home-Drummond,[4] wife of the 6th Duke, who held a number of high positions at Court and was a close personal friend of Queen Victoria; and Katharine Ramsay,[5] wife of the 8th Duke, who became Scotland's first woman

1

Member of Parliament in 1923. It is interesting to note, in the light of Evelyn's later interest, that many of the rooms in Blair Castle bear witness to the fact that throughout the generations women in this family were highly accomplished needlewomen.

In the late 1860s, when Evelyn was born, the landed aristocracy still had great influence in the rural areas as well as leading society both in London and in its country house gatherings. However, times were changing and in all ranks of life free debate of social customs and religious beliefs was replacing the accepted creeds of the early Victorian era.[6] The last thirty years of Queen Victoria's reign saw the beginning of the social and professional emancipation of women, promoted by such people as the philosopher, John Stuart Mill[7] and the educational reformer, Dame Millicent Fawcett, who started fighting for women's suffrage in the 1860s.[8] Gradually, the idea began to gain ground that upper and middle class women, particularly the unmarried, should be trained to support themselves. Since time began, it had been accepted that poor women without husbands or guardians had to keep themselves and their children as best they could, but now there began to be the notion that trained women could be of use to the wider world. Women's colleges were founded at Oxford and Cambridge, and nursing as a serious profession for women advanced after Florence Nightingale's career in the Crimea.[9] Opportunities to widen their horizons came more quickly to the women of the middle class but, in general, aristocratic women still had little with which to occupy themselves, apart from charitable works, visiting friends and relatives, reading and sewing.[10]

Evelyn's early life followed the traditional pattern of a young aristocrat but a severe illness in her teens seems to have triggered a change. Over the next six years frustration and depression made her behaviour gradually become increasingly difficult for her family to accept and the situation came to a head when Evelyn was in her early twenties. She had become obsessed with the study of Gaelic and collecting Gaelic folk tales. She shut herself off from the rest of her family for long hours of study late at night, while her days were taken up with visiting and talking to tenants on the estate. Duchess Louisa felt that her daughter's pursuits were totally unacceptable for one of her class and social status and thus there arose a conflict between, on the one hand, members of the Atholl family and on the other, Evelyn and her desire to fulfil her intellectual abilities. Eventually this conflict resulted in her being removed from the family at Blair.

Later on in her life, responding once more to her environment, she turned to needlework and again worked with great dedication and skill.

2

By then she had become accustomed to an independent lifestyle and was able to follow her interests without hindrance. But the earlier problems left their mark and it proved impossible to achieve a balance between the social expectations of her class and sex and the achievement of her full potential.

Many of Evelyn's letters to members of her family have been preserved in the archives at Blair Castle but, unfortunately, her own papers have not survived. From what we know of her, it is probable that she destroyed correspondence and any diaries she might have had. Although copies were occasionally made by the senders of letters to her, it is of course frustrating not to be able to read the letters she received over the years. This frustration applies particularly towards the end of Evelyn's life when her letters become somewhat rambling. Although research has enabled some queries to be resolved, many questions remain unanswered; for instance, we do not know in detail how Evelyn set about collecting her folk tales or precisely what she intended to do with them, nor do we know who taught her to create such magnificent pieces of embroidery. The paucity of surviving correspondence probably means that we shall never know. Despite the gaps, the family letters which have survived reveal a vivid and fascinating picture of the life of this little known but extra-ordinary Scotswoman.

NOTES

[1] J. Stewart-Murray, 7th Duke of Atholl, *Chronicles of the Atholl and Tullibardine Families*, I (Edinburgh, 1908), 27. [Hereafter, Stewart-Murray (1908)]

[2] K. von den Steinen, 'In Search of the Antecedents of Women's Political Activism in Early 18th Century Scotland: The Daughters of Anne, Duchess of Hamilton' (1990).

[3] B. Henrey, *British Botanical and Horticultural Literature before 1800*, 2 (Oxford, 1975), 584.

[4] Queen Victoria, Unpublished later Journal. When Duchess Anne died in 1897, Queen Victoria wrote 'She is a very great loss to me, as she was such a true friend.' The extract is published by gracious permission of Her Majesty the Queen; V. Mallet, *Life with Queen Victoria – Marie Mallet's Letters from Court 1887–1901* (London, 1968).

[5] S.J. Hetherington, *Against the Tide, Katharine Atholl 1874–1960* (Aberdeen, 1989).

[6] G.M. Trevelyan, *English Social History* (1967), 564.

[7] J.S. Mill, *The Subjection of Women* (London, 1869).

[8] D. Souhami, *A Woman's Place: the Changing Picture of Women in Britain* (1986), 16.

[9] Trevelyan (1967), 562.

[10] A. Bott (ed.), *Our Mothers: Victorian Women 1870–1900* (London, 1932).

1. The Atholl family on the steps of Blair Castle, 1886. (L to R) Duchess Louisa, Lady Evelyn, Lord Tullibardine, Lord James, Lady Dorothea, Lady Helen, Lord George and John, 7th Duke of Atholl. (Duke of Atholl's Collection)

4

CHAPTER 2

Evelyn's Early Years

Lady Evelyn Stewart Murray was born at Blair Castle on 17 March 1868.[1] Her parents, Iain, 7th Duke of Atholl and Louisa, Duchess of Atholl already had two daughters, Lady Dorothea (Dertha) and Lady Helen. After Evelyn the much longed for son and heir was born and he, although christened John George, was always known as Bardie from his title as the Duke's eldest son, the Marquis of Tullibardine. Finally two more sons were born, Lord George (Geordie) and Lord James (Hamish).

The children enjoyed the privileged upbringing of a wealthy aristocratic Highland family. They were cared for by local Gaelic speaking nurses and French speaking governesses, while tutors came to the castle to teach such subjects as Mathematics and German. As well as their scholastic subjects the girls were taught needlework, art, music, and riding and each had a plot of ground which she was expected to tend as a garden. In winter all the children enjoyed skating and hair-raising toboggan rides in the castle grounds while summers were spent at Lundin Links and North Berwick with their governess and servants. The children wrote home to their mother, and their letters – now in the Atholl archives – yield fascinating glimpses of care-free days, playing on the sands, paddling, and exploring; although Dorothea did once complain that at Lundin Links 'there are no bathing machines here and we will have to undress on the sands.'[2] Evelyn's letters reveal her interest in wildlife, the excitement of finding a sea cucumber for the first time and watching a caterpillar spinning its cocoon. However more formal education was not forgotten during the long weeks at the seaside and she wrote of going to the beach one morning to collect shells, adding grumpily 'but we did not go out in the afternoon because we did our lessons so we did not get much by it.'[3]

The Duke and Duchess of Atholl were often away from Blair, attending functions, visiting friends or staying at their London house at 84 Eaton Place. On one occasion eleven year old Evelyn wrote to tell them of an

2. Lady Evelyn Stewart Murray, *c.* 1880. She was then about twelve years old. (Duke of Atholl's Collection)

exceptionally severe storm which destroyed huge numbers of trees on the estate; (the wind) 'blew out a window-pane in our school-room because it was cracked before, and they put out all the gas in the house because the wind always blew it out and they put candles instead and the shutter burst open every minute.'[4] It was 28 December 1879 – the night of the Tay Bridge Disaster.[5]

As the Duke of Atholl's children grew older, the boys completed their education at Eton before joining the Army while the girls spent part of each year with their mother in Eaton Place and were gradually introduced to the round of social events which constituted the London season. Of course this style of life necessitated more dresses and Evelyn's letters become those of a typical teenager, full of complaints about her clothes. She wrote to her mother that she needed 'a pair of three buttoned brown dogskin and cream kid gloves for the ball', adding that she was glad her Swiss frock was too small for her 'because I hate it and hope I've seen the last of it.'[6] Another letter urged her mother not to forget 'the hairpins and the powder.'[7] All three girls were encouraged to become good needle-women and they frequently asked their mother to obtain threads, wool and materials when she was in London, the choice in the local shops being very limited. Christmas and birthday presents were usually home-made and Evelyn's list of requirements for various gifts, written when she was fifteen, shows her attention to detail:

> Please send some of the things that I asked you for, as soon as you can. There is the ribbon for Dertha's pincushion which you did not send with the muslin and lace. . . . I am going to embroider 'Dertha' in what Mlle. calls 'point de feston', she says she does not know the English of it. . . . Mlle. says the scallops (on the name Dertha) are done in buttonhole stitch and they are done on the thick parts of the letters.[8]

In the same letter she also requested fine embroidery cotton and a thimble for a thimble holder, 'a shoe of red plush . . . stuff up the toe and leave a hole for the thimble', maroon silk to line a workbasket, as well as card, gold paint and holland to make blotters for her brothers.

When Evelyn was about fourteen she suffered a severe illness. There is no record of how long she was ill, or even the cause, but in later years her brother Lord James stated that she

> developed what is believed to have been typhoid fever, and for which the condition of the Castle drains was responsible . . . From this date Evelyn developed a certain constitutional weakness.[9]

Whatever the illness had been, it necessitated a very long period of recuperation. Evelyn had always been fond of reading, her sisters regarding her as the bookworm of the family, and now, to pass the weary hours of convalescence, she began to study Gaelic.

The 7th Duke of Atholl was a fluent Gaelic speaker who, owing to his love for the language and his realisation that it was in decline, had for many years fostered the ancient tongue on his vast estate. Gaelic was taught in a number of the schools (despite the objections of some of the school inspectors),[10] local children were encouraged to enter the Duke's Gaelic competition and he insisted that all his keepers, stalkers, ponymen and gillies were Gaelic speakers,[11] as well as the children's nurses and maids. Thus the Duke of Atholl's children were brought up with a good knowledge of the language. Evelyn wrote in Gaelic to her brother Hamish when he was at school in Farnborough, and her father was delighted to correct her letters. He wrote to her in 1884: 'Dear, I can't say how pleased I am to see that you take an interest in the language. It is the one thing I have longed for all your lives, that you should all take a pleasure in learning the language of our forefathers, now alas fast passing away.'[12]

But Evelyn's hobby became an obsession. The long hours of study affected her eyesight, she was told that she required spectacles and was forbidden to read or write by gaslight. She refused to obey. Miss Lanz, the Belgian governess, complained that she no longer had control over her headstrong charge[13] and the Duke and Duchess became concerned about the behaviour of their youngest daughter. To be seen to behave in an acceptable manner was of fundamental importance to the aristocracy of the Victorian era, particularly for an eligible young lady such as Evelyn, who was soon to be presented at court. This event took place in May 1887, when the eighteen year old Evelyn made her début at Buckingham Palace with her cousin Violet Mordaunt. Some weeks before, when both girls were in London being fitted for their ballgowns, the Duke had written to his wife, 'I do hope Evelyn will look well at the Drawing Room. To my mind she is the prettiest daughter we have.'[14]

There was no system of appointments for the thousand or more ladies who would be presented in one afternoon at these socially vital occasions and as Queen Victoria, who loathed these events, usually left after an hour and handed over to the Princess of Wales, the mothers of the débutantes tried to push through their daughters as quickly as possible. The resulting crush was quite horrific.[15] Duchess Louisa wrote to her husband:

8

A fearful Drawing Room ... almost fighting our way, as it was I am afraid Evelyn was very dishevelled as she was squashed at the side of the barriers with part of her gown on the right and the rest on the other – it is really most disagreeable being herded with all those other extraordinary people. I saw exactly four people I knew the whole time.[16]

By way of confirmation, Queen Victoria's entry in her diary that day read 'It was an interminable Drawing Room. I stayed over an hour and then Alex took my place.' But she approved of Evelyn; 'The Duchess of Athole presented her third daughter, also very pretty, and a pretty niece, Miss Violet Mordaunt.'[17]

Meanwhile Evelyn's interest in Gaelic continued to grow and she bought a considerable number of Gaelic books. In the autumn of 1887 she took down a poem from a local Gaelic speaker and her interest in the language must have been well known in the area by this time because a local village bard composed a poem in her honour, praising her love of the people of Atholl and of Gaelic.[18] She might have intended to do more collecting but in October she developed quinsy and diptheria and spent most of the rest of the year with her grandmother in Dunkeld. She was frequently sick and unable to eat, she was plagued by constipation, her eyes bothered her greatly and for a while she was unable to speak. The following spring she was still far from well, her legs were partially paralysed and her hands were stiff. For the first time there was a suspicion that the illness of such an intelligent, highly-strung girl was not entirely physical. Duchess Louisa wrote to her husband, 'Evelyn does not at all seem to think of the cause of her legs – of course there was no doubt that she did have quinsy, though both Doctors said it was diptheriac but not diptheria, but some people have suggested it was "hysterics" which it certainly isn't!'[19]

Evelyn remained weak for a long time, despite the best of medical treatment in Perthshire, London and Kent, where she received galvanisation treatment on her legs.[20] Such treatment had become very fashionable by the latter half of the nineteenth century, when one author stated that it had 'a wonderful therapeutic effect' as a 'stimulant, tonic, sedative, anti-spasmodic and resolvant'.[21] However, Evelyn was not an ideal patient; she would neither take medicine prescribed for her nor eat regularly; she stubbornly refused to go out and her increased desire for solitude and study worried her parents. When Evelyn returned to Blair in May her father was shocked to find how thin she had become and how little she would eat. 'Her weight now is reduced to what it was 7 years ago – she has lost a stone since Xmas.'[22] Her mother still being in London for the season, Evelyn's sister Helen was brought home to act as companion; she reported to Duchess Louisa that Evelyn was improving as she was no longer staying in bed all day. Evelyn greatly resented endlessly being told that she was thin, and would hide when the doctor came to see her. Members of her family by now were aware that although she frequently refused to eat anything, Evelyn would sometimes gorge herself on some favourite food and make herself sick. However, gradually her weight increased to seven and a half stones, her menstrual cycle resumed after a gap of many months and her skin lost its greenish-yellow tinge.

NOTES

1 Stewart-Murray, IV (1908), 481.

2 Atholl Archives, 519. Lady Dorothea to Duch L, 25 May 1878.

3 Ibid., KM166. ESM to Duch L, 31 May 1880.

4 Ibid., KM166. ESM to Duch L, 29 December 1879.

5 See N. Davey, *The Tay Bridge Disaster* (Dundee, 1993).

6 Atholl Archives, KM166. ESM to Duch L, 22 July 1882.

7 Ibid., KM166. ESM to Duch L, 3 October 1884.

8 Ibid., KM166. ESM to Duch L, 5 November 1880.

9 Ibid., 1599.

10 SRO, ED7/1/80. 7th D of A to Scotch Education Department, 29 August 1901. 'Without entering into any discussion as to the circumstances of children in other districts, I am desirous to preserve the Gaelic Language in my own neighbourhood.'

11 Atholl Archives, 423. 7th D of A to Duch L, 29 November 1891. 'I hate the idea of having a non-Gaelic speaking man'; M. O'Murchu, *East Perthshire Gaelic* (Dublin, 1989), 54–57.

12 Atholl Archives, 930. 7th D of A to ESM, April 1884.

13 Ibid., 458. 7th D of A to Duch L, 28 January 1885.

14 Ibid., 470. 7th D of A to Duch L, 7 May 1887.

15 S.P. Fane, *Memoranda of Procedure at Her Majesty's Drawing Rooms and other Ceremonials* (Privately printed, 1895), 3–8; personal letter, Miss K. Reynolds to S. Robertson, 9 February 1991.

16 Atholl Archives, 1657. Duch L to 7th D of A, 13 May 1887.

17 Queen Victoria, *Life at the Court of Queen Victoria 1861–1901* (Exeter, 1984), 20.

18 Atholl Archives, 1474; J. Stewart, 'Luinneag do Lady Evelyn Stewart, inspired by James Stewart's genuine appreciation of Lady Evelyn's love for the people and native tongue of Athole', 25 January 1887.

19 Ibid., 1657. Duch L to 7th D of A, 7 February 1888.

20 A. de Wattville, *A Practical Introduction to Medical Electricity* (London, 1884). Having described the different types of low voltage batteries available, de Wattville gives detailed instructions how to apply two electrodes to the body and gradually turn up the current until a tingling sensation and heat is felt by the patient.

21 G.D. Powell, *Electricity as used in Rheumatism, Gout and Nervous Affections* (Dublin, 1876), Introduction. It was claimed that galvanisation could treat many diverse ailments including nervous debility, rheumatic paralysis, earache, gout, club foot, asthma, bronchitis and croup.

22 Atholl Archives, 421. 7th D of A to Duch L, 14 May 1888.

3. Evelyn aged about twenty-one. Lord James wrote on the back: '1889 or 90. Her hair was cut off after her severe illness in October 1887 – diptheria followed later by a relapse from which she never entirely recovered.'
(Duke of Atholl's Collection)

CHAPTER 3

The Gaelic Years

By the summer of 1889 Evelyn had regained sufficient strength to go on her first trip abroad accompanied by her own maid. She greatly enjoyed staying in Morlaix in Brittany but her letters home were more than a simple record of her visit. They clearly reveal that Evelyn had become fascinated by all forms of Celtic art and way of life. Furthermore, she had realised that the key to making close contact with people who had deep personal knowledge of this ancient culture was to speak to them in their first language. She began to learn Breton and excitedly wrote that she was able to have simple conversations. 'The whole household adores me because I talk to them and am learning Breton. It is wonderful what a difference it makes, just like Gaelic.'[1] While in France she increased her already large collection of books with a number of Breton books, in one of which she made detailed notes of different Breton dialects in the locality.

Back in Perthshire she continued to study and translate poems into Gaelic as well as coaching local children. The Duke of Atholl's Gaelic Competition was held annually in Blair Castle and the Duke was keen that every child enjoyed the day. The winners were presented with handsome prizes; all the competitors were given a framed photograph of a member of the Atholl family and each child who was entering for the first time received an inscribed Gaelic Bible. Evelyn took great pride in the success of her pupils and at least one of them, Christina McDonald, went on to become a noted teacher in Pitlochry and Rannoch and did a great deal to foster Gaelic.[2]

In the spring of 1890 the Duke took Evelyn to Wester Ross for a fortnight. The trip was a great success. The weather was fine, and Evelyn wrote 'I think Loch Maree is the most beautiful place I have ever seen.'[3] She was relaxed and at peace in her own element, but her sunny mood changed abruptly when she had to go to London for the spring season. Her mother, writing to the Dowager Duchess, described how Evelyn was starving herself and had taken to 'walking about all day, generally to Battersea or the Kensington Museum', while drawing lessons failed to divert her as she 'does not get exclusive attention and she often does not go.'[4]

Evelyn's behaviour, particularly her refusal to eat regularly or to attend social functions, may be seen as a desperate cry for help, or a protest against being trapped in a social situation which made it impossible for her to use her intellect. What is clear is that by the summer of 1890 she was suffering severe depression and her failure to fit in with her mother's idea of suitable behaviour created a great deal of friction. One of the major difficulties was that Duchess Louisa had no notion of the nature of mental illness and she unwittingly exacerbated the situation with her authoritarian attitude towards Evelyn. It was at that time fashionable for young ladies to copy out favourite poems and uplifting passages. Evelyn had such a book, but her chosen poems are not the sickly sweet Victorian poems one might have expected from one of her age. A typical example of Evelyn's choice begins:

People do not understand me,
Their ideas are not like mine.[5]

Despite being a fluent Gaelic speaker, Evelyn determined to improve her written Gaelic and it was arranged that Professor McKinnon, who held the Chair of Celtic at Edinburgh University, would set and correct translation exercises for her.[6] By the autumn of 1890 she was preparing to launch herself into a new project, one that would obsess her, and ultimately be the cause of her leaving Atholl. The following year was without doubt the most crucial period in Evelyn's life. Her mental state had begun to deteriorate from the time of her illness some six years earlier, resulting in her suffering spells of deep depression and frustration, but the beginning of the year coincided with Evelyn flinging herself into studies of her own choice. Her torpor vanished and, apart from spells when she was forced to abandon her work, for the next ten months she worked like a thing possessed. By the end of 1891 she had achieved an immense amount of work, but the resulting mental toll was to affect the rest of her life.

From her reading of Gaelic books and periodicals, Evelyn was aware of a growing and fashionable interest in the gathering and recording of folk-lore. The Duke of Atholl and his parents had had a lifelong interest in local history and Gaelic which undoubtedly influenced her, and it seems likely that she was also encouraged by a local photographer and noted Gaelic scholar who lived in Blair Atholl. Paul Cameron, through the Gaelic Society of Perth, worked to promote the language in Highland Perthshire schools, as well as making a valuable collection of poems and stories from his native Rannoch. He and Evelyn co-operated in making arrangements for the Gaelic competition as well as lending books to each other.[7]

Towards the end of February 1891 Evelyn began to collect Gaelic folk tales. Initially she spoke to people in and around Blair Atholl, but later she collected from all parts of the Atholl Estate as well as in Glenlyon, Rannoch, Strathtay and Dunkeld. A number of people, such as the factor and local ground officers, sought out likely sources and sometimes arranged meetings between Evelyn and those Gaelic speakers with knowledge of local traditions and stories. The tales are a fascinating and extremely varied mixture of local history, magic, legend, reminiscences, and snatches of songs. Many are in Perthshire Gaelic and are a valuable record of a form of Gaelic which is no longer spoken. The decline of Perthshire Gaelic, so much regretted by Evelyn's father, is clear to see in local records. For example, the Logierait School Logbook states that the headmaster in 1878 complained bitterly that he had the greatest difficulty in teaching the children because they understood hardly any English, the medium of instruction, whereas by 1913 the headmaster of the same school noted that while a handful of children in his school knew a few Gaelic words or phrases, virtually none of them heard it at home.[8]

In all, between February and November 1891, Evelyn collected 240 tales. She wrote them out very neatly in a number of notebooks, meticulously recording the name of each story teller and the date. Some people, who were particularly good sources of stories, were visited a number of times. Weather, social commitments and health allowing, she went out collecting five days a week, returning home for a quick meal before retiring to her room to work on her notes and books, frequently until four or five in the morning. Sadly none of the surviving papers give any details of precisely how Evelyn set about her collecting in those pre-tape recorder days. We do not know if she noted down all the tales exactly as she heard them or if she altered them in any way, and as we do not have her working notebooks it is not even known if she transcribed all the stories or if she chose only some of them. However, an inkling of her dedication may be gathered from her father's letter describing one of her excursions from Blair Castle to Glen Bruar Lodge:

When she got to the four mile stone they found the road blocked with snow, so she sent the carriage back and walked the four miles to Glen Bruar, and the eight miles back – total 12. It came on to pour with rain and she had no umbrella. When she got back she was so stiff with the wet that she had to get the housemaid to help her off with her things – result loss of voice and bad cold. Is she not a — fool![9]

Duchess Louisa strongly disapproved of Evelyn's enthusiasm for wandering about the estate talking to old folk in their cottages, but the mutual interest in Gaelic created a special bond between Evelyn and her father and this extract clearly shows his amused tolerance of her work, providing it was kept within limits and did not upset Duchess Louisa.

In spring 1891 the Duke and Evelyn again set off together on a trip, this time to the isles of Skye, Harris and Lewis. There she was in her element and even uncomfortable hotels and poor weather could not lessen her zeal. She wrote to her mother, but it is interesting to note that she wrote in much greater detail to her grandmother, and her letters to the Dowager Duchess are brimful of enthusiasm and fun. For instance she wrote of one hotel:

The place was downstairs, exactly opposite the front door, where the inn-keeper was usually loitering about. The door of it wouldn't shut or lock, so you had to leave it half open – with a foot stuck out ready to bang against it if anybody came.[10]

Such conditions were not what the daughter of a duke was used to!

She delighted in speaking Gaelic at every opportunity, noting the different dialects and taking great interest in the old blackhouses which had a peat fire in the centre of the earth floor, the smoke issuing upwards through the thatched roof. While enjoying a walk in Tarbert, Harris, they stopped to look at one, 'a sort of rabbit hole with smoke coming out of it', and to ask about estate boundaries in the area. A very 'clean looking old woman' came to the door and 'immediately greeted me in Gaelic.' They were invited in. 'Inside it wasn't nearly as bad as I had expected, the floor was only turf . . . she was a dear old thing, and showed me her spinning wheel.' Evelyn regretfully had to go, but arranged to visit again the following day. 'We got on famously . . . I am quite delighted with this place!'[11] Both the Duke and Evelyn were pleased to meet 'one of our Gaelic Prize girls, 11 years ago',[12] who had become schoolmistress on Scalpay. Evelyn's one disappointment in Tarbert was that the minister had gone to another island to preach, so she missed six hours of Gaelic psalms and sermons in the local church on Sunday. But it was the kindness of the people, especially the poorest of the crofters, which most affected Evelyn. Years later she recalled that the old woman in the blackhouse had 'insisted on making me a present of eggs which she took out of the bed after having chased the hens away.'[13]

The end of the nineteenth century was a time of great poverty and political upheaval in the Western Isles as well as the mainland northern and western Highlands.[14] When lairds realised that they could make more profit from sheep than from the meagre rents of their tenants, many people were cleared from the land they had traditionally held for generations. Those who did not emigrate were left to eke out an existence as best they could on the poorest land. The Crofter's Act of 1886 did give certain rights to the crofters, but it did not restore the lost lands and in a number of places desperate men were driven to attempt land raids.[15] The Duke and his daughter saw some places where squatters had taken possession of poor and unproductive ground, and although the Duke had no time for radicals, Evelyn wrote 'I shall never abuse the crofters again. I have never seen nicer, kinder or more hospitable people than they are. I will always stick up for them in the future!'[16] Physically and mentally she had been restored by the trip to the Western Isles, and the Duke wrote to his wife 'You would wonder to see the way she ate whilst on her travels.'[17]

On her return to Blair, Evelyn managed to avoid spending the whole season in London with her mother and sisters by staying with her grandmother in Dunkeld for two weeks. Duchess Anne's diary has daily entries such as 'Evelyn collecting old legends', and 'out on her quests.'[18] Evelyn twice went by train to Moulinearn to meet the Middle District Ground Officer who had arranged for a number of good informants to gather together. The following two weeks she spent at Weem, Glenlyon and Rannoch with Egidea Menzies, daughter of Sir Robert Menzies, who guided her to likely sources of tales. In a little over a month, out collecting six days a week, Evelyn added over a hundred Gaelic tales to her collection. When she did eventually join her mother in London, and thus could not continue her work, her behaviour altered dramatically. She refused to go out or eat regularly and this conduct again created tension between Evelyn and Duchess Louisa. It was around this time that the Duchess became concerned about her daughter's increased expenditure. She asked the bank for the reason, but the bank refused to divulge such information, even to the Duchess of Atholl. In fact, Evelyn's money was being spent on books in Scots and Irish Gaelic, Breton and Manx. Within a few years she had acquired over 450 books, mainly Gaelic religious and literary works, many of them first editions. A long time later, in 1958,

George Iain Murray, 10th Duke of Atholl, presented them to the National Library of Scotland, as the 'Blair Collection'.[19]

A few days after Evelyn arrived in London a number of Scottish newspapers, including the *Constitutional* and the *People's Journal*, printed a short article on the Atholl family and Gaelic. Having detailed the ways in which the Duke of Atholl was encouraging the language, the article continued:

> Lady Evelina Murray ... is at present preparing a graded reading book in Gaelic which will, it is expected, give the people a more intelligent acquaintance with Gaelic, and enable them to speak, read and write it. Lady Evelina Murray is a highly proficient Gaelic scholar – speaking, reading and writing the language with great fluency and precision.[20]

While this resulted in letters of praise and encouragement from many people, including the eminent Gaelic scholar Alexander Carmichael (1832–1912), who addressed her as 'a fellow worker in Gaelic literature',[21] others must have been less enthusiastic. Evelyn wrote to her sister Helen,

> That beastly book of mine ... I am so bothered about it ... I particularly dislike people thinking that I am doing that ... when there are people far more capable of doing it than me. I only hope the contradiction will get into the Oban Times.[22]

Duchess Louisa also made sure that the fact there was to be no book came to the ears of one or two gossips on the estate who could be relied upon to spread the tale. But word of arguments in the castle seeped out and some people on the estate whispered that the Duchess had put Evelyn's book on the back of the fire.[23]

However it is clear that Evelyn had collected Gaelic stories with some intention of ultimately publishing them because, in 1939, very near the end of her life, she made certain that her precious manuscripts were passed into the care of Professor Carmichael Watson of Edinburgh University, 'whose grandfather, Dr Carmichael, was so interested in my work. It is my desire that both the letters and the mss. should be published for public circulation, not less than a year after my death.'[24] At the same time she told her brother Hamish which of her photographs she wished to be used as the frontispiece. Unfortunately, the stories were not published because Professor Watson was drowned in action in 1942, and in 1958 the Duke of Atholl gave the manuscripts to the School of Scottish Studies in

Edinburgh. The archivist there, Dr Alan Bruford, has stated that the Lady Evelyn Stewart Murray Collection is of value from several different aspects:

> Among a good number of Gaelic folktale collections from late nineteenth-century Scotland it is the only one made by a woman, the only one to cover West Perthshire, the only one from which nothing was printed in the collector's lifetime, and the only one that gives a proper idea of the richness and variety of the repertoire of both supernatural and historical legends, as well as longer folktales, to be found in one area. In fact it is a remarkably wide area to have been so effectively combed in a single year, by someone working under exceptionally difficult conditions and with little professional help or instruction. [25]

Evelyn was very unhappy in London in the summer of 1891, and her behaviour became increasingly difficult. Their Graces had for some time feared that Evelyn might have inherited some mental instability. One of Duchess Louisa's sisters, Harriet Mordaunt, had been declared insane during a divorce case which was the *cause célèbre* of its day, [26] and an uncle of the Duke had committed suicide after years of mental imbalance. Wishing to do everything possible to help their daughter, the Duke and Duchess discreetly sent Evelyn to Buxton in Derbyshire, under the name Miss Murray. There she remained for six weeks under the care of Miss Isles, an experienced minder of highly strung young ladies. One of the Duke's letters reveals some of Evelyn's trauma as he tried to reassure her that 'no one thought or thinks you mad.' He ended the letter by assuring her that he was pleased that she was so fond of Gaelic, 'but for goodness sake be reasonable, and don't refuse to do nothing but work at Gaelic all day and night. It is overstudy, not all study, that is objected to.' [27]

A letter from Duchess Louisa, who had no Gaelic and appears to have made no effort to learn what was still the first language of the majority of the people on her husband's estate, reveals that she approached the situation from a very different viewpoint from that of her husband:

> I like you to go amongst the country people, if you do so for the sake of their good, but you must remember that it is equally your duty to associate with your equals ... when you return home do try and conquer yourself and to live at peace with us all. [28]

But Evelyn bitterly resented being sent away to Buxton under supervision. She secretly destroyed clothes which were sent to her, took to keeping her belongings in a locked case below her bed and finally refused to return home in time for the Gathering. This meeting, the principal social event of the year in Atholl, was held each September in a field near the castle and local people flocked to see the Highland games which were enjoying a fashionable revival at that period. In the evening a dinner was held in the Atholl Arms Hotel, the spacious dining room having been specially built for the purpose. The Duke and Duchess always invited a large number of their relations and friends and it was quite unthinkable that any member of the Atholl family would fail to attend.[29]

Miss Isles was able to view her charge's behaviour more clearly and with greater comprehension than Evelyn's own family and it is in one of the reports which she sent to Duchess Louisa that real understanding and a practical idea for helping Evelyn to cope with her problems are to be found. She suggested that a ladies college, such as Girton or Newnham, both at Cambridge, would perhaps allow Evelyn to use her brain 'wholesomely' and allow her to discover 'that all is not bliss in doing as you like ... It is so sad to see a bright young life going wrong.'[30] Miss Isles's suggestion was ignored, and one is left wondering what Evelyn Stewart Murray might have achieved had her intellectual abilities been harnessed, trained and encouraged.

Evelyn returned to Blair a few days after the Gathering, but refused to attend Hunt Balls, which she had enjoyed in previous years, or even to stay with her grandmother in Dunkeld. Her behaviour became increasingly bizarre and she began to spend most days in bed, refusing even to have it made, although she did occasionally go out to collect more Gaelic tales. On one of her outings she fell and broke a garden key and she sent an amusing letter to her brother Hamish, complete with thumbnail sketches.[31] It is a measure of her fragile mental state at this time that whilst she was capable of writing a light-hearted letter to her youngest brother she was refusing to speak to her family at Blair Castle, and days of starvation were interspaced with occasional bingeing on favourite foods. Her mother was at her wits' end as to what to do with her.

The local doctor, Robert Irvine, puzzled long and hard over the case. Because detailed medical notes are not available – if they ever existed – it is impossible now to state with any degree of certainty precisely what ailed Evelyn but it seems to be very likely that bulimia and anorexia nervosa were involved. The eminent London physician, Sir William Gull, had first used the term anorexia nervosa as early as 1874, stating that 'the want of appetite is, I believe ... due to a morbid mental state.' He noted that young women suffering from this complaint were especially liable to

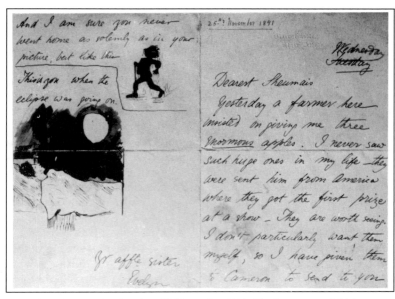

And I am sure you never went home as solemnly as in your picture, but like this—

This is you when the eclipse was going on.

Yr apple sister
Evelyn

25th November 1891

Wednesday
Tuesday

Dearest Sheumais

Yesterday a farmer here insisted on giving me three *enormous* apples. I never saw such huge ones in my life—they were sent him from America where they got the first prize at a show— They are worth seeing. I don't particularly want them myself, so I have given them to Cameron to send to you

4. Evelyn's letter to her brother, 25 November 1891. The latter part of this year was a deeply traumatic time for Evelyn, yet she wrote this delightfully illustrated letter to James, then at school in Farnborough. (Atholl Archives, 930)

this morning— so I hope they will arrive safely.

When I fell & broke the key, I didn't look half as comfortable as the picture you did of me. I was like this— Then I rolled about— in agony in all sorts of position

Then I crawled home like this, feeling very sorry for myself

I think when you slipped in the water, you must have been like this & then

this happened

Or perhaps it was like this — I think this must have been more like it. It is rather like you, particularly the ears. don't you think so. Then you got up.

'mental perversity' and a degree of hyperactivity which was quite remarkable considering that they would, at the same time, rapidly become
increasingly emaciated.[32] This appears exactly to describe Evelyn's
condition. It is interesting to note that Dr Irvine and Dr Gull must have
had contact at one time because the Pitlochry doctor possessed a silver ink
stand inscribed 'To Dr Robert Irvine M.D. 1887. In grateful recognition
of much kindness during a time of great anxiety. Dr Gull.'[33] It is possible
that Dr Irvine was in touch with Dr Gull at this worrying time, seeking
advice, but no evidence for this has been found. However, even Dr Gull
had no definite treatment for the ailment and Dr Irvine felt that Evelyn's
condition was now so serious that she should go right away for some
time. He feared that her condition might deteriorate even further if she
remained at home, and in all probability he thought that her removal
would also reduce the pressure on the rest of the family, particularly
Duchess Louisa. He suggested a cruise to Australia or New Zealand, but
the family feared that Evelyn was now so seriously ill that she might throw
herself overboard on a long sea voyage. Duchess Louisa, however,
was adamant that Evelyn was not to stay in Britain where she might be
recognised and cause embarrassing questions to be asked.

Despite repeated warnings from her parents and grandmother that her
conduct could not be tolerated, Evelyn's mental state made her incapable
of grasping the seriousness of her situation. Duchess Louisa was herself
beoming ill with the worry of trying to cope with a daughter who seemed
determined to cut herself off from the rest of the family. Letters to her
husband and mother-in-law show the Duchess's frustration and growing
anger.[34] Her patience was exhausted and she became increasingly
resentful towards Evelyn, whom she blamed for the strain which was
sapping her own strength. Evelyn paid no heed. By the end of November
1891 the Duke and Duchess were very reluctantly making arrangements
for her to go to Switzerland to stay under the care of a lady who was very
highly recommended to them.[35] Miss Emily Murray MacGregor, the
Dowager Duchess's cousin and companion, would accompany her on the
journey; over the coming years she was to act as a faithful and discreet
intermediary between the Atholl family and Evelyn.

Plans were made for Evelyn to leave Blair Atholl quietly on 15 December and she was told to pack and prepare for the journey. But on that
morning Duchess Louisa wrote a distraught, barely legible note to
Emily Murray MacGregor, cancelling the arrangements because 'There
has been a terrible scene.'[36] Later the same day Dr Irvine wrote to
Dunkeld with more details. After numerous delays during which Evelyn

obdurately refused to pack, she eventually appeared wearing 'strange boots and no cloak' despite the snow which was on the ground. She refused to get into the waiting coach and walked part of the way down the drive with the doctor taking her arm, Duchess Louisa and Helen riding in the coach a few yards behind. Suddenly 'she turned and came to the carriage door; and then putting off all reserve, seized hold of the wheel so that if it moved she would break her arm . . . the fact is that there was a struggle.' The only servant present was the coach-driver and it is a measure of the Atholls' desire to avoid any possibility of scandal that a relieved Dr Irvine reported that the scene was 'very brief and no spectators and no loud noises.'[37] Evelyn was led back to the castle.

Her final act of defiance left her exhausted; her spirit was finally broken. That night she wrote to her mother a brief note on a torn scrap of paper, 'If I may stay till Saturday I will go quietly – I have a lot of things I wish to arrange.' On the back of the paper, in Duchess Louisa's hand, is the inscription 'From E – 5 p.m. 15th Dec. 91. Written in pencil but traced over by me in ink. L A.'[38] Years later the bitterness was still with Evelyn when she wrote to her brother Bardie of this time:

> One of the last things Mama ever told me was that I was not fit to be in the house with any of you . . . I was told I would not even be allowed to remain in the country. I daresay I might have given every-body the plague if I did.[39]

Five days before Christmas 1891, twenty three year old Evelyn left her home, Blair Castle. She would not return.

NOTES

[1] Atholl Archives, 421. ESM to Duch L, 25 June 1889.

[2] Personal conversations with S. Robertson, 1992–3.

[3] Atholl Archives, KM166. ESM to Duch L, 2 April 1890.

[4] Ibid., 501. Duch L to Dow D of A, 26 May 1890.

5 Ibid., 1372. Poetry book of ESM, vol. V.

6 Ibid., 1472. ESM's Gaelic lessons, Nov. 1890 – Sept. 1891.

7 P. Cameron, 'Perthshire Gaelic Songs and their Composers', in *Transactions of the Gaelic Society of Inverness*, XVII and XVIII (Inverness, 1891 and 1893).

8 Logierait School Log Books, Headmasters' reports (1878 and 1913).

9 Atholl Archives, 423. 7th D of A to Duch L, 1891.

10 Ibid., 1653. ESM to Dow D of A, 18 April 1891.

11 Ibid.

12 Ibid.

13 Ibid., 429. ESM to JSM, 26 June 1938.

14 J. Hunter, *The Making of the Crofting Community* (Edinburgh, 1976).

15 Ibid.

16 Atholl Archives, 1653. ESM to Dow D of A, 18 April 1891.

17 Ibid., 423. 7th D of A to Duch L, 25 April 1891.

18 Ibid., 647. Dow D of A's diary, 8 and 14 May 1891.

19 National Library of Scotland, Blair Collection. The collection consists almost entirely of religious and literary works in the various Celtic languages, the greatest number being in Scottish Gaelic.

20 Atholl Archives, 1467. Article in the *Constitutional*, 17 June 1891.

21 Ibid., 1474. Alexander Carmichael to ESM, 3 July 1891.

22 Ibid., KM166. ESM to Lady Helen, July 1891.

23 Private conversation with S. Robertson, autumn 1991.

24 Atholl Archives, 492. ESM to Prof C. Watson, 26 June 1939.

25 Personal letter, Dr A. Bruford to S. Robertson, 10 September 1992.

26 E. Hamilton, *Old House at Walton: More about the Mordaunts* (Salisbury, 1988); Atholl Archives, 1667. Reports on the Mordaunt Divorce Case 1870.

27 Ibid., 63. 7th D of A to ESM, 3 August 1891.

28 Ibid., KM166. Duch L to ESM, 23 August 1891.

29 Ibid., 634. Newspaper cuttings about the Atholl Gathering.

30 Ibid., KM166. Agnes Isles to Duch L, 5 September 1891.

31 Ibid., 930. ESM to JSM, 25 November 1891.

32 I. Loudon, 'Chlorosis, Anaemia and Anorexia Nervosa', in *British Medical Journal*, 281 (December 1980).

33 Private conversation with S. Robertson, spring 1993.

34 Atholl Archives, KM166 and 163. Duch L to 7th D of A, Nov. and Dec. 1891.

35 Ibid., 480. Duch L to Mrs O'Grady, 4 December 1891.

36 Ibid., 480. Duch L to E MacG, 15 December 1891.

37 Ibid., 480. Dr R. Irvine to E MacG, 15 December 1891.

38 Ibid., KM166. ESM to Duch L, 15 December 1891.

39 Ibid., KM83/1. ESM to M of T, 11 August 1903.

24

CHAPTER 4

Montreux to Malines

Montreux was a popular and fashionable resort for the wealthy, the air being considered highly beneficial to invalids and convalescents. Evelyn was taken to stay with Mrs O'Grady, a lady with considerable experience of difficult and nervous young ladies, who leased an entire floor in the Hotel Monney, a middle class hotel set between much grander establishments. While the front of the hotels faced La Grande Rue, windows at the rear overlooked the small gardens of each hotel, the promenade, and Lake Geneva.[1] The Duke and Duchess had tried hard to find a suitable, discreet and attractive place where their daughter could convalesce before returning home, but Evelyn's bitterness at being sent away from home would become lifelong. In her later years she recalled Mrs O'Grady's third floor apartment, complaining that the stone stairs were like servants' stairs, that her room had no outlook and that she had nothing to do all day but 'stare at the flies on the ceiling.'[2] In her disturbed mental state, then and in later years, Evelyn's account of events was not always accurate, a point that had to be borne in mind while researching her life. In this instance, letters from Mrs O'Grady to Duchess Louisa make clear that Evelyn had plenty of diversions. Twice weekly lessons in French and German were arranged, as were daily walks and frequent coach and boat trips to beauty spots and places of interest. As soon as another of her young ladies left, Mrs O'Grady offered Evelyn a much more attractive room overlooking the lake, but she refused.[3] Despite Mrs O'Grady's best efforts, Evelyn hated Montreux. She wrote to her grandmother, 'I really think that I shall go out of my mind if I stay here much longer.'[4]

Her mental state improved radically, however, when she had the idea of moving to Brittany. She asked her sister Helen to send out a number of her Gaelic and Breton books, and she ordered more from booksellers in France. In Brittany she felt she could continue her work of collecting folk tales and Mrs O'Grady was delighted in the change that had come over her. But the Duke and Duchess refused to let her go[5] and Evelyn suffered severe depression for many weeks. While still in very low spirits she received an ultimatum from her mother which offered a stark choice – to come home at the end of July 1892 and 'try to be like other people'[6] or to remain with Mrs O'Grady. Evelyn stubbornly refused to go home. Mrs O'Grady wrote sadly of her charge's 'brilliant mind clouded with weeds of self-reliance, pride, independence and narrowness.'[7]

Evelyn was taken by Mrs O'Grady to the mountains for some weeks in the summer, but the change of routine and a fear of being forced to meet Miss Murray MacGregor, who was then travelling on the Continent, severely unsettled her. Sleepless and irritable, she began to starve herself again; light and heat affected her and she objected to even the smallest change such as a book or table being moved. When they returned to Montreux the local physician, Dr Tidey, stated that the basic problem was that of self starvation, and he warned that any illness could be fatal.[8]

On 15 December 1892 Evelyn's eldest brother Bardie, the Marquis of Tullibardine, had his 21st birthday. Guns were fired at Blair Castle, followed by toasts and speeches at the door, and the presentation of gifts by deputations of tenants and officers of the Atholl Highlanders. In the evening a grand ball was held followed by a display of fireworks, while huge bonfires blazed atop many of the principal hills throughout the Atholl estate.[9] It had been hoped that Evelyn would return to participate in the celebrations for her brother's majority, but she flatly refused to do so, and again slumped into a deep state of depression. She seems to have taken some interest in embroidery at this time as she bought patterns and threads from local wool shops and had some embroidery lessons,[10] and for a while she studied Welsh,[11] but her spirits remained low. She avoided all contact with the other young ladies in the apartment and, Mrs O'Grady wrote, 'her pride is deeply wounded because she is in a middle class milieu ... day by day she is trying to break all communication with us.'[12] Many years later Evelyn wrote that her time in Switzerland almost destroyed her, both physically and mentally:

> You see all my energies and my affections were centred in my home and country and to have been deprived of everything at one blow would have been too much for anyone. Mama had of course no sympathy with my pursuits, but they surely did no harm to anyone, and some people liked them.[13]

By spring 1893 Mrs O'Grady was openly voicing a fear that Evelyn might commit suicide. Duchess Anne, the Duke, and Duchess Louisa all admitted that they each, for some considerable time, had secretly harboured the same fear.[14] They decided that Evelyn must return home by June, leaving the choice of date to Evelyn herself. Plans were made and belongings packed, but at the last moment Evelyn, now severely emaciated, retired to her bed, and her departure was postponed.

Mrs O'Grady's time in Montreux was coming to an end as her lease expired, and she decided to go to Belgium where her mother lived. Evelyn again refused to return home to Blair and in August 1893 went instead with Mrs O'Grady to Brussels; but her condition there deteriorated to such an extent that the family feared she would have to be committed to an institution. A doctor who was a specialist in mental illness, Dr de Smeth, attended Evelyn for some time and he felt that a slow cure could eventually be achieved if Evelyn were taken away from everybody she had known while she was ill.[15] Mrs O'Grady resented his instrusive and intimidating manner and feared that any failure of his might be blamed on her, but Evelyn's parents were desperate to do everything possible to assist their daughter back to health, and they decided that his advice should be followed.

After a series of delays, Evelyn finally moved to Laeken, a suburb of Brussels, in March 1894.[16] Although Dr de Smeth had now taken over official responsibility for her, she was assured by Mrs O'Grady that the latter would come at once should she ever be needed. Emily MacGregor continued to look after practical matters and to act as intermediary between Evelyn, the doctor and the family. The next two and a half years would remain troubled and unsettled but, with the move to Laeken, Evelyn slowly began to build a new life for herself. She enjoyed the freedom of walking in the nearby park and was soon asking for new boots. Turning to needlework with renewed interest, Evelyn asked Emily to make arrangements to send her tambour frame and requested that a handkerchief edged with Brussels lace, which she had sent as a birthday present to her grandmother, should be returned to her so that she could embroider it.[17]

At the end of April Emily failed to persuade Duchess Louisa, who was unwell at the time, to go to Brussels in order to gain first hand knowledge of the people who were caring for her daughter. Soon plans were being made for Evelyn's middle brother, Geordie, to visit her but she continued to be resolute in her determination not to see any member of her family; the doctor, too, advised against the visit, believing that 'it would throw her back.'[18] Dr de Smeth thought that plenty of exercise would help to keep Evelyn's nervous nature in check, and by late summer Emily was able to report that he had succeeded in bringing Evelyn into better health.[19]

In the autumn Duchess Louisa told Dr de Smeth that she was most anxious that Evelyn should come home for the wedding of her elder sister which was to take place early the following year. Evelyn, however, not only declined an invitation to be Dertha's bridesmaid but also refused to go to the wedding, although she did send a gift of a Brussels lace fan. As a result of this stubborn attitude Evelyn was to spend the day of the wedding in tears, alone in her room. Her mother then made what was to be her final attempt to encourage her daughter to come home, suggesting that if Evelyn did not wish to come for the wedding she should come later; the Duchess thought that it was time for her to return and take up her position again as a daughter of the house. But Evelyn still remained in Belgium. A few months later, while on a visit to Brussels, Dertha and her husband called to see Evelyn. When she heard them coming she locked herself in her room but agreed to talk to her sister through the closed door, saying that she had vowed never to see any of her family.[20] Eventually, having promised not to go in, Dertha was able to persuade her to shake hands round the door. Mrs O'Grady expressed the opinion that 'it is no case, but a dogged pride and despair. God only knows why the poor child should harden herself against the only people she cares for.'[21] Dr de Smeth still hoped that, in time, Evelyn would return to her family but Emily's prescient view was that Evelyn would never return home: 'I think she will have sufficient good sense to guide herself without a doctor's supervision, and in two or three years at all events could choose her lodgings and where she would like to live.'[22]

Encouraged by the doctor to keep herself occupied, Evelyn arranged to have lessons in embroidery and Brussels needlepoint lace. She described how, in her early experience of such work, she used a stool to prop up her knees to hold the embroidery frame. Fine needlework had captured her imagination and it was not long before she was asking for paintings which she could adapt as designs for embroidery. At the same time she asked if the 150 francs a month for her embroidery could be increased to 200 as she had a new, and more expensive, teacher. A few weeks later, however, she explained that

> it is not the actual lessons which come expensive – and I have got the French person to take less by saying I would take a good many lessons – but that does not make any difference, it is the accessories and materials and designs which come extremely expensive.[23]

5. The three sisters at Blair Castle, *c.*1888. (L to R) Helen, Evelyn and Dorothea. (Duke of Atholl's Collection)

Unfortunately for the historian, Evelyn was never forthcoming about the people who taught her embroidery and lace-making, and their identity remains a mystery. It is intriguing that estate gossip at Blair consistantly whispered that she 'went abroad and went to a convent'.[24] Lace making was, and still is, taught in some Belgian convents and it is perhaps not too fanciful to wonder whether Evelyn might have learnt at least some of her needlework skills from a nun. Further evidence that hints at this possibility is to be found in the tone of the testimonials of her work (in Chapter 5), some of which sound as if they might have been written by a religieuse.

Although she had some funds of her own from a legacy received from a great-aunt,[25] Evelyn now began to overspend, mainly on carriages and embroidery. Her grandmother came to the rescue and, for the first time, Emily had the task of explaining to Evelyn the facts about her financial position. Evelyn promised to keep within her limit in future and it was not long before Emily was writing to express her approval of Evelyn's grasp of her financial affairs.

In the autumn of 1895, determined to get away from Laeken, Evelyn persuaded Mrs O'Grady to accompany her on an expedition. Travelling south they stayed for a few weeks at the Hotel des Bains in Chaudfontaine but, finding it extremely cold in the Ardennes, they decided to move on to Bruges.[26] From here Evelyn visited Ghent and decided that she would like to spend some time there; a suitable apartment was found and arrangements made for her to live with a companion from the New Year. Her father agreed that an allowance of £30 a month would be paid to her and this sum was to include everything except the companion's salary of £6 a month. For the first time Evelyn was to manage her own day to day financial affairs and she said that she would like to use any spare money for embroidery. Mrs O'Grady, sure now that Evelyn was quite able to manage, returned to Brussels. At the time of Evelyn's move to Ghent Dr de Smeth reported that physically her health was good; the paralysis of one leg had almost disappeared, her weight was normal and, although her appetite was capricious, meals were eaten regularly. Her time was occupied and daily life had become normal.[27]

Perhaps as a gesture of defiance, Evelyn kept her address in the Rue Miry secret from her family, leaving them to find out from Mrs O'Grady or the doctor. She employed a girl to do the domestic chores and reported to Emily that she was being very good about money and had not driven at all in Ghent! Evelyn was, however, determinedly spending a considerable amount of money on gold and silver embroideries, the beginning of what would become over the next twenty years a fine collection of lace and embroidery from all over the world. She was quite prepared to be frugal in other ways, sometimes with necessities, in order to indulge her passion for needlework. However, when she was living at Laeken Evelyn had bought a parrot to keep her company; writing to Emily one day from Ghent she sent the following message for her youngest brother Hamish:

> (The parrot) is very tame and says a few words – it always wants to perch on my shoulder or on my head and pulls out my hair pins.[28]

Coco was to be her constant companion for the next twenty-five years. She was heartbroken when he died, and when Bardie kindly offered to send her another parrot Evelyn begged him not to, because it was 'not a question of <u>a</u> parrot but <u>my</u> parrot which was my child.'[29]

After six months in Ghent Evelyn returned to Mrs O'Grady's house in Brussels where, a few weeks later, she received an unexpected visit from Bardie. When she saw him 'she was off like a shot',[30] but they did have quite a long talk through a closed door before Evelyn started to cry and her brother thought it better to leave. Soon afterwards Emily, while staying in Brussels with the Dowager Duchess, was reassured by Dr de Smeth that Evelyn was well in every respect.[31] Towards the end of the summer, however, Mrs O'Grady became concerned that Evelyn had worked herself up into one of the attacks of nervousness to which she was prone. The fact that she was now making some import-ant decisions about her future way of life probably contributed to this relapse. Evelyn's companion had recently recommended an apartment in Malines, a town midway between Brussels and Antwerp, and had taken Evelyn there to see it. Soon afterwards Evelyn reported to Emily that she had taken the lodgings in Malines, adding that she supposed 'Malines will be as well as anywhere else. I don't much care where it is, it is all one to me.'[32]

The Duke, exasperated by this news, declared that he would not make any extra payments and these would not be incurred if Evelyn did not keep changing her place of residence. He now insisted that she had to manage on £25 a month and no more, apart from £5 a month for the companion, as long as she had one. By this time Duchess Louisa no longer had any confidence in the doctor's hopefulness and now appeared resigned to Evelyn's remaining abroad. She wished to help her daughter at this time with a gift of ten pounds, but Evelyn's less than gracious response was that she would accept what was given for maintenance but

31

she did not want any presents. All the evidence points to the fact that, despite the many efforts by members of her family to communicate and persuade her to return home, Evelyn's pride was so wounded that her resolution never seriously wavered. She was unyielding and adamant that, whatever the cost, she would remain abroad in exile.

NOTES

1 In the later twentieth century the Hotel Monney was demolished and the resulting gap-site attractively landscaped to provide pedestrians with a pleasant walkway from La Grande Rue to the promenade. [Information from the Montreux Archivist]

2 Atholl Archives, KM83/1. ESM to M of T, 11 August 1903.

3 Ibid., KM166. Mrs O'Grady to Duch L, 3 February 1892.

4 Ibid., KM166. ESM to Dow D of A, 18 January 1892.

5 Ibid., KM480. Dow D of A to ESM, 2 February 1892.

6 Ibid., 501. Duch L to ESM, 20 February 1892.

7 Ibid., KM166. Mrs O'Grady to Duch L, 20 April 1892.

8 Ibid., KM166. Dr S. Tidey to Dr R. Irvine, 29 September 1892.

9 Stewart-Murray, IV (1908), 511.

10 Atholl Archives, KM166. Mrs O'Grady to Duch L, 19 October 1892.

11 Ibid., KM166. Mrs O'Grady to Duch L, 3 November 1892.

12 Ibid., KM166. Mrs O'Grady to Duch L, September 1892.

13 Ibid., KM83/1. ESM to M of T, 11 August 1930.

14 Ibid., 425. Dow D of A to 7th D of A, 9 March 1893.

15 Ibid., KM166. Dr de Smeth to E MacG, 7 October 1893.

16 Ibid., KM166. Mrs O'Grady to Duch L, 22 March 1894.

17 Ibid., 487. ESM to E MacG, 9 June 1894.

18 Ibid., KM166. E MacG to Duch L, 10 June 1894.

19 Ibid., KM166. E MacG to Duch L, 4 August 1895.

20 Ibid., KM166. Lady Dorothea Ruggles-Brise to Duch L, July 1895.

21 Ibid., KM166. Mrs O'Grady to E MacG, 11 October 1893.

22 Ibid., KM166. E MacG to Duch L, 10 January 1895.

23 Ibid., 487. ESM to E MacG, 24 February 1895.

24 Private conversations with S. Robertson, spring 1993.

25 Atholl Archives, 63. ESM to 7th D of A, March 1898.

26 Ibid., 487. ESM to E MacG, 18 November 1895.

27 Ibid., KM166. Dr de Smeth to E MacG, 16 January 1896.

28 Ibid., 482. ESM to E MacG, 10 March 1896.

29 Ibid., 508. ESM to 8th D of A, 20 July 1919.

30 Ibid., KM83. M of T to Duch L, July 1896.

31 Ibid., KM83/1. E MacG to Duch L, 12 July 1896.

32 Ibid., KM166. ESM to E MacG, 25 September 1896.

6. La Rue du Bruel, Malines, c.1905. Evelyn lived at no. 73 – approximately half way down the left hand side – from 1896 to 1914, and from 1920 to 1923. (Collection of Mr Marcel Kocken, Malines)

34

CHAPTER 5

The Embroidery Years

Evelyn arrived in Malines, a quiet Flemish-speaking town famous for lace-making, on 8 October 1896.[1] Her rooms in the Rue du Bruel included a large and bright sitting room, a bedroom and a kitchen; she was pleased that she could go into the garden – which was crammed with fruit trees – as much as she wished. There were two elderly English ladies who also lived in the same house but Evelyn rarely saw. them as she was soon busy studying; it was not long before she added Flemish to her knowledge of languages. Mrs O'Grady visited her from time to time but Dr de Smeth's services were soon dispensed with, and a few months after arriving in Malines Evelyn was telling Emily that she had never been so comfortable since she had been away from home.[2] With her independence now established, her family became concerned that she should keep herself to herself. Emily was quite confident that she could be trusted to do so and, in support of her opinion, quoted these words from Evelyn:

> I think you know me well enough to know that I have no inclination
> to do what I should not do. If I had wished to I should have done so
> long ago. That is the one reason why I have kept aloof from everyone
> – I know absolutely no one except two or three governesses.[3]

Although Evelyn would have a succession of servants and companions, her attitude and the consequent restrictions were to make her life one of secrecy, solitude and increasing loneliness. Her mental problems probably made it difficult for her to cope with people, and for many years her only friends were her paid companions. From the moment she was sent abroad it had been agreed that she would be known as 'Miss Murray' and, throughout her life, she would go to extreme lengths to conceal her true identity. She avoided speaking to British people when she was away from home and never acknowledged that she knew people and places in Scotland mentioned in conversation. Family photographs were never displayed but kept hidden away in a drawer.

Evelyn proved her ability to manage her own affairs, and from 1898 she was given an allowance of £340 a year, paid quarterly; in addition, her father made a payment of £5 a month to her companion. Emily's role as go-between had come to an end but she and Evelyn continued to correspond regularly. On one occasion Evelyn admitted to Emily that it was her own decisions and actions that were responsible for the way her life had turned out. She confided that she often thought of the past, and that when she was 'down in the dumps'[4] she could not even read.

As many women have done throughout history Evelyn found solace in embroidery; it was to be her main occupation and would absorb a great deal of her time for the next eighteen years. Along with her childhood, these were probably the best years of her life. Just as her Gaelic studies had once been, needlework became a total commitment and was mastered with consummate skill. Margaret Swain, the distinguished needlework historian, describes Evelyn as 'perhaps the most outstanding needlewoman of recent times.'[5] She was born at the beginning of a most interesting period in the history of embroidery as it entered a new and expanding era. The Industrial Revolution had created a middle class of women who, like upper class women, had plenty of time to devote to such activities. In Scotland, whilst the technically perfect Ayrshire whitework flourished as a cottage industry,[6] for the leisured classes the most popular type of embroidery was Berlin woolwork, a form of canvas work.

From the time of the Great Exhibition in 1851 there was an increasing awareness of the importance of good design. In 1872 the School of Art Needlework, which continues to flourish as the Royal School of Needlework, was founded 'for the two-fold purpose of supplying suitable employment for Gentlewomen and restoring Ornamental Needlework to the high place it once held among decorative arts'.[7] Other schools with the same aims were soon started, notably the Wemyss School of Needlework in Fife, and – three years after Evelyn left Scotland – what was to become a famous and innovative embroidery department at the Glasgow School of Art.

Evelyn, however, was hardly touched by any of these influences and does not fit comfortably into any category. Her embroidery is a personal and creative result of circumstances; whilst remaining traditional, it is also unique. It was worked on a large frame which was too cumbersome to take away with her and she often complained that she got very bored on wet days away from home. Some of her work was inspired by pieces in her collection and she would work a sampler in the same technique with complete assurance. A geranium leaf worked very finely in an old technique called 'or nue', in which metal threads are laid and couched over the surface of the fabric, was the result of her study of angels in two Viennese pictures in her collection. When the weather was very hot and it was impossible to embroider, because the heat from her hands would have spoilt the work, Evelyn would try some drawing instead, or play the flute which had been one of her extravagances during her time in Brussels.

In the autumn of 1898 Evelyn travelled to Venice and Vienna, the first of several such journeys that she would make in the following years. There was virtually no contact now with members of her family but in the summer of 1899 Bardie married Katharine Ramsay, always known as Kitty, and during their honeymoon the couple called on Evelyn. However, her attitude had not changed and once again she locked herself in her room. Hamish had written to her from time to time but, apart from sending him the occasional message, Evelyn first wrote a letter to him when he was serving in South Africa during the Boer War:

> I was not much older than you when I left home and you will have been able now to feel a little of what I felt when I left Blair, only when I left, I knew I was never to return, which I hope you will do before long.[8]

When Duchess Louisa became ill in 1902 Evelyn wrote to her for the first time; a brief letter in which she said 'I have been very sorry to hear that you have been so ill, if you will only get well again soon, I shall be very glad.'[9] She received a reply from her Mother but this letter has not survived. That spring the Duchess and her eldest daughter went to Italy, where her health deteriorated, and in July she died. Evelyn was overwhelmed and, as always, opened her heart to Emily expressing her anguish at her mother's death.

> If I could have seen Mama and spoken to her and kissed her once it would have meant at least peace of mind to me at last, now it is gone for ever.[10]

Emily believed that had Duchess Louisa lived she would have returned home via Belgium.

This period was one of great emotional strain for Evelyn, and after her mother's death it was almost two years before she did any more embroidery. When she became ill while staying at Laeken in the spring of 1903 her sister Helen came to look after her, and that summer Bardie came to visit her and she met her sister-in-law for the first time. Efforts were made once again to persuade Evelyn to return to England, but she vigorously rejected them all. By this time she had certainly become accustomed to living on the continent and had evolved an acceptable way of life for herself. There might still have been an element of stubborn pride in her decision but at that time Evelyn believed that she and her family could no longer have anything in common and said 'It was settled so by Mama and so it must remain.'[11] Recalling past times, she told Bardie that she had 'taken up embroidery more or less – it is quite a harmless employment and I don't think this time anyone can have anything to say against it.'[12] This is a unique reference to her interest in and commitment to embroidery and she rarely mentions in letters anything about the work that filled so much of her time. From this point contact was resumed and friendship restored between Evelyn and her brothers and sisters, although it was not until after the First World War that they corresponded and saw each other regularly. Evelyn always thought that her father had 'simply sacrificed'[13] her and, although she now agreed to write to him occasionally, she did not wish to see him and they never met again. After Evelyn's companion Stephanie became ill with tuberculosis and returned to her home in Austria, Evelyn went to see her, and stayed for two months in Vienna, where Stephanie died. Her position as companion was taken by her friend, Hermine; a quiet person, she remained with Evelyn for eight years.

Evelyn often went to the Royal Museum of Art and History in the Parc Cinquantenaire in Brussels. This museum has a fine collection of lace and embroidery and she became acquainted with its director, Eugene van Overloop, who was an internationally known expert on lace.[14] From time to time it was also Evelyn's custom to send her work to the principals of an embroidery school, to seek their advice and 'to ask what they thought of it'.[15] Unfortunately there is no record of which schools these were, but a translation of a testimonial from one of them reads: 'I cannot adequately praise the beauty of the working of this . . . no pupil of ours has ever produced work so beautifully done in every detail as yours is. We are all delighted with it.'[16]

One of the most significant years in Evelyn's life was 1905, when she and her companion started to embroider the British Arms, first trying out all the stitches on another piece of material. Evelyn made a rough sketch of the design but it was drawn out in detail by a draughtswoman in Vienna. Most of the ideas were Evelyn's and the design of the arms was taken from the back of an old photograph taken by W. & D. Downey. Many portraits of the Atholl children had been taken by this well known studio, who were photographers to Queen Victoria.[17]

7. The British Arms (15″ × 17¾″). Evelyn's embroidery was declared by the Royal School of Needlework to be 'the finest of its kind known'. (Atholl Archives, KM82)

When she was an old lady Evelyn recalled how she came to embroider her masterpiece.[18] One day, in a beautiful shop in Brussels, she had bought for her collection an embroidery of the Belgian Arms worked in white with lace stitches. This purchase gave her the idea of having an embroidery made of the Atholl Arms. The College of Arms in London provided an illustration and the shop selected one of their best needle-women to do the embroidery. However, when the piece was completed and brought to the shop the shopkeeper was not at all impressed and refused to accept it, saying that the work was very badly done; the woman was so angry that she seized her embroidery and tore it to pieces! It was this episode that inspired Evelyn to learn to do this particular kind of very fine embroidery herself, and the result was the 'British Arms' which took several years to work and was completed in 1912. While the panel was still unfinished Evelyn sent it to an embroidery school for an opinion and the following is a translation of their assessment of her work: 'The fine embroidery which you do is perhaps the most artistic thing to be found anywhere and you must realize this and be glad that it is so.'[19] The incredible fineness of the completed work is considered by many to be the most beautiful and accomplished panel of whitework in Britain and probably the finest example of modern British embroidery.[20] Margaret Swain believes that

> If all embroidery of this century were to be destroyed, and this one piece, like St Cuthbert's stole in Durham Cathedral, were to be the sole survivor of its age, it would offer mute, heraldic evidence of the excellence of British embroidery in the twentieth century.[21]

The charming and elegant design is embroidered in soft cotton on fine cambric in satin stitch and stem stitch, and the delicate drawn fabric fillings reflect Evelyn's knowledge of the technique of Brussels Point de Gaze lace. The British Arms are enclosed in a scroll border decorated with roses, thistles and shamrocks, with the Prince of Wales's feathers and motto 'Ich Dien', at the lower centre.

It is interesting to note that while she was working on the British Arms, Evelyn took the time to do some needlework with a more practical use and made a waistcoat for Bardie, just as she used to do when he and Geordie were schoolboys at Eton. Amazingly, it was not until 1913 that Evelyn started to wear spectacles; but by then her embroidering years were coming to an end. It became increasingly difficult for her to do the very fine work in which she delighted and she would never have compromised by lowering her standards; as she said some years later 'I do hate amateurish work in every department.'[22]

Emily's long letters to Evelyn continued until the former became ill in 1912 and eventually had to have a nurse to look after her. Evelyn was very concerned about the health of the woman who had befriended and supported her for over twenty years. As well as a link with home, she was from the same social background; someone whom Evelyn could meet on equal terms and in whom she could confide with complete trust. At Evelyn's suggestion, when Emily celebrated her eightieth birthday, the family gave her a present of a specially made brooch which contained strands of hair from each of them. Although she was still only forty, Evelyn's hair was almost white, but she managed to find a few strands of brown hair for the brooch.

When she was forty-two Evelyn seems to have gone through a short period of mid-life depression; she wrote to Emily 'to try to get it out',[23] describing how she felt, 'so old and done for and once one is forty one feels one is going downhill.'[24] Shortly before this time, while staying in the country for the summer, Evelyn had met a doctor from Antwerp and they had arranged to visit each other when the holiday was over; but the doctor became ill and died soon afterwards. Evelyn said sadly that she seemed fated never to make a friend. This attempt at friendship might have been the result of her mental state at that time, because it was certainly contrary to her usual attitude to people. Although it would seem to be out of character and an isolated occurrence, the experience certainly contributed to her low spirits. There were also several domestic upheavals in Evelyn's life at this period; first her companion left and then her maid, who had been with her for many years, married. However, towards the end of 1913 Evelyn had the good fortune to employ a young woman called Mathilde Caulier who came from the small Belgian town of Peruwelz near the French border.[25] Her marriage had been unhappy and she had left her husband and come to Malines with her small daughter, Sidonie.[26] Capable and hard working, Mathilde was twenty-eight years old and would remain in her employment for the rest of Evelyn's life.

NOTES

1 Domiciliary Register, Malines City Archives.

2 Atholl Archives, 482. ESM to E MacG, 7 March 1897.

3 Ibid., KM166. E MacG to Duch L, 26 December 1896.

4 Ibid., KM83. ESM to March of T, 12 September 1909.

5 M. Swain, *Historical Needlework – a Study of Influences in Scotland and Northern England* (London, 1970), 113.

6 See M. Swain, *The Flowerers: the Story of Ayrshire White Needlework* (1955).

7 B. Morris, *Victorian Embroidery* (1962).

8 Atholl Archives, 489. ESM to JSM, 15 January 1900.

9 Ibid., KM166. ESM to Duch L, 20 May 1902.

10 Ibid., 64. ESM to E MacG, 21 July 1902.

11 Ibid., KM83. ESM to M of T, 11 August 1903.

12 Ibid.

13 Ibid.

14 Academie Royale des sciences, des lettres et des beaux-arts de Belgique, *Biographie Nationale* (Brussels, 1965), 568.

15 Atholl Archives. Embroidery notebooks of ESM. [Evelyn devised a method of identifying each piece in her collection. She used the letter 'B', from the old word 'broidery', for the embroidery she collected; 'BE' for her own work; 'L' for the lace she collected; and 'LE' for her own lace work, each followed by a number.]

16 Ibid.

17 The Duke of Atholl's Collection, Blair Castle.

18 Atholl Archives, KM85/2. ESM to 8th D of A, 29 January 1938.

19 Ibid. Embroidery notebooks of ESM.

20 Ibid., KM82. 9th D of A to Duch K, 4 December 1955.

21 Swain (1970), 113.

22 Atholl Archives, 528. ESM to JSM, 30 January 1921.

23 Ibid., 66. ESM to E MacG, 19 December 1910.

24 Ibid.

25 Domiciliary Register, Malines City Archives.

26 Atholl Archives, 508. ESM to 8th D of A, 22 December 1918.

CHAPTER 6

The War – and Peace at Last

In July 1914 Evelyn, Mathilde and Sidonie set off for a holiday in the old Belgian town of Spa, famous since the sixteenth century for its baths and mineral waters. Evelyn had rented the Villa des Gardes, a small house hidden in woods away from the main road. It belonged to the Comte de Chastel who lived at the nearby Château de la Havette, the largest and finest property in Spa, and Evelyn was allowed to walk in the grounds whenever she liked. A local farm provided milk and eggs.

Evelyn's name appears each day in *La Saison de Spa*,[1] the official list of foreigners staying in the town, until publication ceased on the eve of the First World War. When the Belgian government refused free passage to German troops through Belgium to France, Germany invaded Belgium. Although the soldiers passed through Spa they left the town untouched and it was one of the few places where there was no fighting. The postal services no longer operated and it was several weeks before Evelyn's family received news of her through the bankers in Brussels. Some letters were still getting through to Spa, however, and Evelyn knew that her brother Geordie had been reported missing. She feared that there could be little hope for him and it was learnt later that he had been killed in France. At the beginning of the war Evelyn occasionally had the opportunity to send letters by messenger. She wrote to Emily, enclosing a general letter to be circulated round the family; her letter ends poignantly, 'Goodbye, dearest Cousin Emily and I hope that we shall be able to correspond again in better times.'[2] But this was not to be as Emily died in 1917. Evelyn also had the chance to return to Britain via Holland, and the family sent money for this purpose, but again she chose not to do so. She did, however, make arrangements to get a passport for Mathilde in case it should become necessary for her to leave, as she would never have done so without Mathilde and Sidonie. As hostilities continued many thousands of Belgians were given shelter in Britain, but Evelyn and her household remained in Spa throughout the war.

43

8. Evelyn 1914. She wrote to Tullibardine: 'Enclosed my pretty passport photograph in case you should admire it – it was taken end 1914 – my hair has grown white since. The English doctor [Cafferton] who died here [Spa] guessed that I was the same age as he was – he was 63 (I was then 46). When I saw this pretty photo I told him I forgave him as I looked about 70 if I was like that'. (Atholl Archives, 508)

It was some time before Evelyn found out that Malines had suffered badly and had been heavily bombarded on three occasions; many of the inhabitants had fled. She realised how lucky she was to be in Spa but feared that her house in Malines had been destroyed. Evelyn had taken advantage of an opportunity to become acquainted with the Burgomaster, being well aware that he was the most influential person in Spa, and was therefore able to tell him of her concern about what had happened in Malines. Because as Burgomaster he was able to travel freely, he offered to go to look at her house, and from him she learnt that her rooms were severely damaged and beautiful china statuettes were smashed 'not even to bits but to powder.'[3] He also reported that the Director of the museum in Brussels had been in Malines a few days earlier and kindly taken Evelyn's collection of lace and embroidery to be stored in the museum. A few weeks earlier a Belgian lady, whom Evelyn did not know, had called on her and offered to arrange to have some letters sent to England by messenger. Evelyn had sent two letters, one to Emily and one to Mr van Overloop at the museum in Brussels, authorising him to enter her flat in Malines and take charge of her lace and embroidery; both these letters were left open according to instructions. However, instead of delivering the letter to Mr van Overloop, the messenger had impersonated him, gone to the house in Malines, stolen much of Evelyn's collection and taken it to a house in Brussels. He then travelled on a false passport to England where he is believed to have sold some of the lace. On his return this man called on Evelyn introducing himself as 'Mr de Fault', a Frenchman living in the Rue van Artevelde in Brussels. He told her that as he had not had time to go to the museum before going to England he had read the letter to Mr van Overloop and then gone himself to Malines and taken some of the lace and embroidery as he did not consider the museum to be a safe place. But he refused to say where he had put Evelyn's work.

Greatly alarmed, Evelyn obtained a pass to travel to Malines and visit her apartment. There the caretaker confirmed that de Fault had visited the house, introduced himself as the director of the museum and shown her Evelyn's signature at the end of the letter. He had then taken all the lace and embroidery that he could cram into a small cardboard box. The caretaker had been told that Miss Murray wished her to take the rest of the articles and store them in her house, for which she would be handsomely rewarded. All were now being stored in the damp cellar of a café-bar, among them the 'British Arms'; fortunately Evelyn had arrived in Malines before the thief could return to take them away. Evelyn then obtained another pass enabling her to go to Brussels to see Eugene van Overloop. Together they went to the house in Rue van Artevelde where de Fault refused to say where he had put the lace and embroidery, but agreed to bring the pieces to the museum a few days later; he failed to do so. After repeated efforts Mr van Overloop eventually obtained the box only to find that about eight pieces, all finished articles of great value, were missing. Mr van Overloop then kept the collection safely stored away in the museum until the war was over.[4]

Although Evelyn, Mathilde and Sidonie remained in Spa in relative safety, the war years were a time of hardship and deprivation for everyone, with little food, heat or light. Evelyn found the want of light especially trying, but what she longed for most during those bleak days was a large hot water bottle. 'You can't think how frugal we have become,' she wrote afterwards.[5] In 1915 when the British doctor died, Evelyn became the only British person in Spa. Throughout the war she received only very occasional letters from Britain and one, which Kitty was able to send through friends in June 1917, did not reach her until September. It was then that she learnt that her father had died nine months earlier and that her sister Helen had married. During 1918 Spa saw much of the closing German moves of the war when the General Headquarters was established there.[6] The Kaiser, who had been living at a château near Spa, abdicated on 9 November and two days later the armistice was signed.

A few weeks later Evelyn was overjoyed to receive visits from both Bardie and Hamish, the latter having been interned in Holland after he was wounded and taken prisoner in December 1914. The family could now send parcels of food, clothes and medicines to Evelyn and she said 'I only wish I had had a quarter of your good things last year when everyone was reduced to fighting for a vinegary German loaf at any price.'[7] Mathilde and Sidonie opened each parcel with squeals of pleasure and Evelyn made herself sick tasting the contents. She asked Hamish to send tobacco and cigarettes for two friends of hers who were craving for them. But amid all the rejoicing Evelyn was very upset when she learned that her landlord in Malines had died, and thought how sad it was that so many old people had not been able to hold out until the end of the war. Evelyn was full of praise for Mathilde, who had been such a support to her, and told Bardie that her servant cooked quite well, sewed beautifully, was a very good housemaid and 'seems to have all the qualities rolled into one.'[8] Mathilde had made a vegetable garden in very bad, stony ground and in Evelyn's opinion cultivated it better than most gardeners. No photographs of Mathilde have been found but we are fortunate to have a description of her as she was in 1940. She is remembered as being a small, stout countrywoman who was always dressed in black, with ankle length skirts. Very protective of Evelyn, she had the determined walk of a strong-minded person, her footsteps usually being heard before she was seen![9]

After the war a German military mission remained in Spa in conference with the allies. Evelyn was pleased when Hamish went to Spa as a member of the prisoner of war department of the Armistice Commission, and brother and sister were able to see each other frequently and dined together most days.[10] When the Commission finished its work Hamish was posted to the British Mission in Brussels.[11] However, Evelyn was by now far from well; the years of austerity had taken their toll. She suffered from neuralgia, her eyes were inflamed and she was having problems with her teeth. That autumn she went to Brussels where she stayed for over three weeks while receiving treatment from her oculist and dentist.[12] She was very glad though to have the opportunity to see her good friend Eugene van Overloop again. A few weeks earlier she had been 'quite enchanted'[13] when she heard from him that the man who had stolen her lace was now behind bars for other crimes. Soon after her return to Spa Evelyn met her brother-in-law, David Tod, when he and Helen visited the town. The following spring Dertha went to Spa and the sisters met again for the first time since they had shaken hands round the door at Laeken so many years before. Visits from the family were complete when Hamish took Kitty to see Evelyn. Kitty had feared that her sister-in-law might be nervous as it was such a long time since they had met, so she planned to talk continuously in order that Evelyn did not have to converse, but the ploy backfired and Evelyn afterwards asked Hamish if Kitty 'always talked without stopping.'[14] Both women were very musical and it was hoped that Kitty might have influence on Evelyn and, in time, persuade her to return home. Evelyn however found it all quite exhausting and 'took two days holiday in bed'[15] after Kitty's departure!

By this time Evelyn had given up her idea of taking a house in Malines and decided instead to return to her old rooms there. That autumn the weather was beautiful as she picked the last of the greengages before she, Mathilde and Sidonie returned to Malines. A few weeks later the work of the British Mission in Brussels came to an end and Hamish returned to Scotland.[16] New Year 1921 was celebrated in Malines with several roisterous days of drinking, singing and dancing. Evelyn did not take part in any of this merrymaking, but she did receive a love-letter from Eugene van Overloop, and commented that 'he never gets any further!'[17] Five years later she was saddened by the loss of her old friend who died suddenly from a heart attack only a few months after retiring from the museum. Evelyn's health did not improve and she continued to have treatment from the oculist and dentist in Brussels; most of her time was now spent in either receiving treatment or recovering from it. A tear duct became troublesome and the tears would pour down her face.[18] Unfortunately the therapy was not successful and, beginning to despair, she reluctantly agreed to go to Edinburgh for medical treatment, on condition that no one outside the family would know; she would continue to be known as 'Miss Murray' and not go anywhere beyond Edinburgh.

The appropriate arrangements were made and on 20 December 1921, exactly thirty years to the day since she had crossed the Channel on her way to Switzerland, Evelyn returned to Britain. She travelled immediately to Edinburgh, where she stayed with Helen and David, and was seen by several doctors, who decided that all her teeth should be removed as they were believed to be poisoning her gums and the cause of her bad health. Afterwards Evelyn described herself as 'a cross between a slobbering baby and a jibbering old woman'[19] and spent much of her time mourning her teeth. A few weeks later she went into a nursing home in Edinburgh; her usual weight was only just over six stones but by this time it had gone down to a mere five stones eleven pounds.[20] The doctors now decided that her ill health had not, after all, been caused by her teeth, but by colitis which had produced painful inflammation all over her body. On hearing this diagnosis Evelyn was extremely cross and complained bitterly that having her teeth out had only resulted in her being further handicapped, but she enjoyed the rest and care that she received in the nursing home and particularly appreciated the water mattress on her bed. Members of the family visited Evelyn frequently during her stay in Edinburgh. Much to their amusement she was a voracious reader of any advertisements she came across and this resulted in many requests being made to Dertha, who patiently accepted these commissions. Having nothing much to do in Edinburgh, Evelyn was able to indulge this pastime more than ever and Dertha was asked to obtain hats, moth-proof bags and special glue for repairing china.

The doctors decided finally not to perform an operation on her tear duct and Evelyn began to make plans to return to Belgium. In May a very excited Mathilde travelled to Edinburgh, and at the end of the month she and Evelyn returned to London to catch the boat-train for Brussels. A few weeks later they went to spend the summer at Spa.[21] When the house in the Rue du Bruel was sold in the summer of 1923 they moved into a property in the nearby Rue Louise, which was bought in Mathilde's name.[22] Many of the houses in Malines were in a very bad state of repair as the owners had done little to them since the war, and Evelyn and Mathilde had to spend more than a year getting their house in good order. 'Always waiting for workmen who never came',[23] they sometimes wondered if the work would ever be finished. As the only Flemish speaker in her household Evelyn had to do all the talking to the men who came to repair, paint, hang paper, upholster and lay linoleum.[24]

By this time Evelyn and her sister-in-law Kitty had become firm friends and, both being highly intelligent women, enjoyed discussing many things with each other. When, in the General Election of 1923, Kitty became the first woman to be elected to parliament by a Scottish constituency,[25] Evelyn wrote to congratulate her, although her feelings about the event were mixed. She thought that Kitty's election would not make Bardie's life any more comfortable and felt sad that the couple would no longer be able to spend so much time at Blair. Significantly one of the things that Evelyn said she would dislike about the life of a politician was 'that one had constantly to adapt to the times.'[26] She once said that she 'had no ambition to be a suffragette'.[27] In spite of her independent life-style and self sufficiency, many of Evelyn's attitudes remained firmly rooted in the Victorian period of her youth. Her life went on quietly and uneventfully in Malines; her greatest wish now being to spend her remaining years in some degree of comfort. Her days were taken up with gardening, reading and music. Gardening seems partly to have taken the place of embroidery and become an outlet for her creativity. She wanted to make 'a pretty garden'[28] and when Hamish said that he would come to help she made arrangements for a nurseryman and a jobbing gardener to be there at the same time. Roses were among her favourite flowers and she made a special study of them; she always had bowls of flowers in the house and used to make pot-pourri from rose petals. Evelyn was also very proud of the grapes grown in her unheated greenhouse. One Christmas Day she described how they had roses on the table and ate the last of the year's grapes, which were sweet and delicious.[29]

Evelyn had other hobbies; always a keen and serious reader, she diligently read the liberal Belgian newspaper *Étoile Belge* and followed current affairs closely. After the war the family regularly sent her magazines such as *Country Life* and the local Perthshire newspapers which she read avidly. She enjoyed an opportunity to discuss books; her favourite contemporary writer was A.C. Benson, but she also appreciated the works of Philip Gilbert Hamerton.[30] Of Kitty's book on Russia, *The Conscription of the People*, it was characteristic of Evelyn to say that 'It's a book that can only be read in small doses, to digest it thoroughly, so it has taken me a long time.'[31] A proficient pianist, as she grew older she spent more and more time at her piano, and always found great pleasure in going to Brussels to listen to piano recitals, which she much preferred to orchestral concerts. Her favourite music included the works of Saint-Saëns, Liszt and Chopin.[32] She no longer travelled abroad, but each year returned to Spa, often in the spring, which she said was the time she always missed Blair. Always fond of the natural world, Evelyn spent much of her time at Spa in the garden and was delighted one day when she identified nineteen different species of birds there. This experience prompted her to describe the garden as 'the birdiest place'[33] she had ever seen. Over the years Mathilde and Sidonie had gradually become her family and Evelyn was always very concerned about their welfare. On the few occasions when Mathilde was ill, Evelyn did her best to help her and would sometimes arrange a holiday for her afterwards. When members of Evelyn's own family called on their way home from holidays, they would occasionally bring gifts for Evelyn's household. Once, returning from Italy, Bardie and Kitty brought a Venetian leather bag for Mathilde and a purse for Sidonie, which Evelyn later reported were kept as treasures.[34] When Sidonie became engaged to be married, Evelyn told Hamish that a present would be much appreciated and suggested 'perhaps a little brooch that she can pass on to her descendants.'[35]

As the years went by Evelyn's thoughts turned more and more to Scotland, and she would recall with perfect clarity people, places and events of the past. Sometimes when she wrote the date on a letter it would bring back a memory and she would remark how, in the old days, she always looked forward to the Atholl Gathering or, on the twelfth of August, wonder if they were shooting grouse that day.[36] These tranquil years after the war had helped to restore Evelyn's health, and when Dr Sinclair visited her in 1931 he reported to Helen that he found her in good spirits and thought that she looked in better health than in Edinburgh in 1922, although his opthalmoscope revealed signs of cataract in both eyes. Three years later when Helen died, having survived her husband by only a year, Evelyn wrote 'She did so much for me and there was so little I could do for her . . . If I could believe in re-union beyond the grave I should feel that she is happy now.'[37] But Evelyn did not have any religious faith and had no belief in a future life; her philosophy of life was to live and let live.

50

Many years earlier Evelyn had assured Bardie that her collection of needlework would remain with the family; in 1936, when Blair Castle was about to be opened to the public for the first time, it was agreed that it should be displayed there for visitors to see. Evelyn now began to prepare her lace and embroidery and to make arrangements to send it to Blair in the cupboards which she had had specially made for it. Under a recent finance act, licences for the duty-free importation of goods intended for 'the advancement of art'[38] could be issued. It was acknowledged by the authorities that, on the grounds that they were 'to be exhibited in the museum at Blair',[39] Evelyn's collection was covered by the legislation. The embroidery and lace, insured for two hundred and fifty pounds, finally left Antwerp on 29 October 1936 on the S.S. *Chrichtoum* bound for Dundee. There were terrible gales at sea and Evelyn was very anxious about 'the embroidery boat'.[40] Typically, she had given instructions that the family should not write until much later but that, when the things had been delivered, a wire should be sent to her saying simply 'Arrived safely'.[41]

Her embroidery notebooks, kept in the archive at Blair, contain information about each item in her collection, and instructions about storing and displaying them; as Evelyn said 'everything is noted in them.'[42] She often included the advice that 'this must be looked at through a magnifying glass.'[43] One piece of work is evocatively described as being tarnished through working by lamplight, while another has become yellow as a result of being partly worked in the open air. Needles, threads, scissors and beautiful old books of samples of thread are still kept, carefully labelled, just as Evelyn left them in the cabinets. The collection of over one hundred and twenty items, more than half of them worked by Evelyn, can still be seen at Blair Castle in an exhibition which is changed regularly.

9. Sampler of linen embroidery (BE5). Patterns of counted thread embroidery worked with silk thread. Evelyn said: 'A fine canvas needle must be used so as not to prick into the linen thread. It will be interesting to look at the back because two (squares) on the back are not worked through but passed with the needle on the front only.'
(Embroidery notebooks of ESM) [see note 15, p. 42]

NOTES

1 *La Saison de Spa* (1914). [Bibliothèque Communale de Spa]
2 Atholl Archives, 109/2. ESM to E MacG, 25 November 1914.
3 Ibid., 109/2. ESM to her family, 25 November 1914.
4 Ibid., 526. Account of theft by JSM; ibid., 508, ESM to 8th D of A, 10 March 1919; ibid., 93. ESM to Miss Osborne, 16 January 1937.
5 Ibid., 526. ESM to JSM, 13 January 1919 (6.30 p.m.).
6 J. Hammerton (ed.), *World War 1914–1918: A Pictorial History* (London, 1919), 1284, 1534.
7 Atholl Archives, 526. ESM to JSM, 13 January 1919 (9.30 p.m.).
8 Ibid., 508. ESM to 8th D of A, 22 December 1918.
9 Oral account given to S. Robertson in March 1992 and February 1994 by Mrs Jean Forest, Pitlochry, who met Mathilde Caulier at Easter Moncreiffe in 1940.
10 Atholl Archives, KM82. JSM to Duch K, 15 March 1919.
11 Ibid., 526. ESM to JSM, 5 September 1919.
12 Ibid., 526. ESM to JSM, 9 October 1918.
13 Ibid., 526. ESM to JSM, 5 September 1919.
14 Ibid., 527. ESM to JSM, 6 August 1920.
15 Ibid.
16 Ibid., 527. ESM to JSM, 10 October 1920.
17 Ibid., 528. ESM to JSM, 4 January 1921.
18 Ibid., 508. ESM to 8th D of A, 6 March 1921.
19 Ibid., 508. ESM to Lady Dorothea Ruggles-Brise, 14 January 1922.
20 Ibid., 484. ESM to Lady Dorothea Ruggles-Brise, 24 March 1922.
21 Ibid., 529. ESM to JSM, 28 July 1922.
22 Ibid., 491. ESM to JSM, 5 January 1935.
23 Ibid., 529. ESM to JSM, 19 August 1923.
24 Ibid., 528. ESM to Lady Dorothea Ruggles-Brise, December 1923.
25 K.M. Murray, *Working Partnership* (1958).
26 Atholl Archives, 93. ESM to Duch K, December 1923.
27 Ibid., 93. ESM to Duch K, November 1924.
28 Ibid., 529. ESM to JSM, 2 September 1925.
29 Ibid., 530. ESM to JSM, 30 December 1929.
30 P.G. Hamerton, *Human Intercourse* (1910); P.G. Hamerton, *The Intellectual Life* (1910).
31 Atholl Archives, 93. ESM to Duch K, 17 June 1932.
32 Ibid., 491. ESM to JSM, 19 January 1936.
33 Ibid., 529. ESM to Lady Dorothea Ruggles-Brise, 10 March 1923.
34 Ibid., 528. ESM to JSM, 16 May 1921.

[35] Ibid., 530. ESM to JSM, 17 May 1927.

[36] Ibid., 529. ESM to JSM, 19 August 1923; ibid., 530. ESM to JSM, 12 August 1927.

[37] Ibid., 93. ESM to Duch K, 26 December 1934.

[38] Ibid., KM83. The Custom House, London EC3 to 8th D of A, July 1936.

[39] Ibid.

[40] Ibid., 93. ESM to Duch K, 2 November 1936.

[41] Ibid., KM83. ESM to Miss Osborne, 12 October 1936.

[42] Ibid., embroidery notebooks of ESM.

[43] Ibid.

CHAPTER 7

Home to Atholl

Evelyn's health now began to deteriorate and she said sadly that 'to be old and alone is a terrible thing.'[1] She suffered from neuritis and was plagued by insomnia, for which she tried several remedies, of which 'Medinal' was the most effective.[2] In December 1937 Dertha died suddenly while staying in the south of France and when Evelyn was told of her sister's death she had a severe nervous collapse. Bardie went immediately to Malines where he found her, confused and lonely, huddled up in a dark corner. The following day she appeared to be much better and told her brother that, on reflection, she would like to go to England.[3] However, Evelyn insisted that Mathilde could not be a servant and said that they would go to London as two friends, Miss Murray and Madame Caulier. Certain that she saw a second invasion of Belgium, and not wishing to be caught there again, Evelyn decided to leave Malines before the preparations for her return had been completed. She sent a telegram to Hamish and temporary accommodation had to be found for them in a lodging house.[4]

A few weeks later Evelyn and Mathilde moved into a newly built flat in Wimbledon.[5] Furniture was bought from a local department store, but Evelyn's bed had to be returned to the shop because the springs were not as she had ordered.[6] As a result, for the first few nights in her new home, she slept on a mattress on the floor with a parasol to keep out the light! Bardie and Kitty visited Evelyn and sometimes, as a treat, would bring a melon for her; Hamish went to Wimbledon whenever he was in London. Evelyn's thoughts now became more and more often centred on her collections. One day she wrote to Hamish to ask him to look for her Gaelic books in the library and to see where her collection of embroidery and lace was at Blair.[7] She never went out at Wimbledon and spent much of her time in bed; she wrote fewer and fewer letters and gradually Mathilde took over the task of writing to Hamish. Evelyn, continuing to read the newspapers which Mathilde went out to buy for her every day, became depressed by the possibility of war and, as it appeared more and more likely, her sadness and quietness increased.

On 24 June 1940 London had its first air-raid warning, and four days later Hamish took Evelyn and Mathilde to the safety of his home at Easter Moncreiffe; after almost fifty years, Evelyn had returned to Perthshire. Hamish recorded in his diary that she was 'still well and very happy',[8] but over the next few weeks her condition worsened. She grew much weaker and had a slight stroke, followed a week later by another, after which she never fully regained consciousness. On 30 July Hamish was with her when she died peacefully at five o'clock in the morning.[9]

Evelyn was buried at Tirinie, beside her sister Helen and within sight of her old home at Blair Castle, 'amongst the hills and the heather which her heart had never forgotten.'[10] Six estate workers were invited to join Bardie and Hamish in carrying the coffin, each one representing a sister or a wife who had been one of Evelyn's Gaelic pupils fifty years before. After the simple ceremony a piper played a Gaelic air. 'It was one which Evelyn liked, a song the title of which rendered in Gaelic is "My faithful fair one".'[11] Years later the daughter of one of the pall bearers recalled that her father had spoken in awe of a beautiful swan which was seen that day on the tiny lochan beside Tirinie, reminding the Highlanders of the ancient Celtic belief that a swan was once a soul.[12] Evelyn's death was announced in *The Times* and a few people still remembered her; one of them wrote to Hamish 'How well I remember her blue eyes, and her delightful smile, indeed she was attractive.'[13] All that Evelyn had was left to Mathilde who remained at Easter Moncreiffe until the end of the war. Afterwards she returned to Belgium where, after selling the house in Malines, she went to live in Spa.[14]

NOTES

[1] Atholl Archives, KM83. ESM to 8th D of A, 1936.

[2] Ibid., 93. ESM to Duch K, 7 March 1934. [Medinal was made by a German company, Schering AG (now Schering Health Care). Its main ingredient was barbitone sodium, a barbiturate with sedative and hypnotic properties, which is no longer used.]

[3] Ibid., KM83/2. 8th D of A to JSM, 15 January 1938.

[4] Ibid., 492. ESM to JSM, 3 May 1938.

[5] Advertisement for flats at Emerson Court, Wimbledon Hill Road in the *Daily Telegraph*, 11 December 1936.

[6] Atholl Archives, 492. ESM to JSM, 19 June 1938.

[7] Ibid., 492. ESM to JSM, 20 November 1938.

[8] Ibid., 945. Diary of JSM.

[9] Ibid.

[10] Ibid., 955. JSM to William Moncreiffe, 13 August 1940.

[11] Ibid.

[12] Private conversation with S. Robertson, summer 1993.

[13] Atholl Archives, 981. Letters of condolence to JSM.

[14] Ibid., 996. Mathilde Caulier to 9th D of A, 25 August 1949.

CHAPTER 8

Conclusion

It is very difficult to put Lady Evelyn Stewart Murray into the general context of female achievers in the Victorian era because she does not neatly fit a convenient, conventional mould. Library shelves are crammed with books on splendid women such as Emily Davies,[1] Beatrice Webb,[2] and Caroline Norton,[3] but it is clear that such women came from a very different background from Evelyn's. They were born into middle and upper middle class homes and they had to strive long and hard to gain entrance to the public sphere which was essential to their achieving their aims, such as improving women's education, extending workers' rights and gaining legal rights for married women. Female aristocrats of the same period did not need to forge a path into the public realm, they were born into it. From earliest childhood their role in life was clearly set out. Following a limited education they would make a successful marriage, produce heirs and give moral support to their husbands by being perfect society hostesses. A few, who were so inclined, did 'good works'. Baroness Burdett-Coutts, for example, was an extremely wealthy woman who was concerned about the effects of poverty and overcrowding in parts of London and her philanthropy supported new housing schemes, evening classes and social clubs, as well as a huge variety of other charitable causes in Britain and abroad.[4] However, most aristocrats kept their public work on a much more modest scale. One example is the Duchess of Rutland, who gave encouragement during fund raising for the building of the Birnam Institute near Dunkeld,[5] and produced a book of uplifting articles such as 'Gathering Flowers and Scattering Comforts' and 'The Art of Doing Kindness in the Kindest Manner'.[6] It was perfectly acceptable for aristocratic women to be seen publicly, and sometimes very ostentatiously, undertaking such activities.

The three daughters of the 7th Duke of Atholl had ideal aristocratic role models in their mother and paternal grandmother. Duchess Louisa was one of the seven Moncreiffe sisters who were all celebrated beauties.

She was completely at ease with and totally fulfilled by the seasonal round of grand balls, house parties and foreign travel. The Dowager Duchess Anne was an archetypal aristocrat, but she had wider interests. She successfully combined a very full social life, which included regular attendances at Court where she was a Lady of the Bed-chamber and a close personal friend and confidante of Queen Victoria,[7] with an interest in the well-being of the Atholl tenants. In 1854 a school for girls, together with a teacher's house, was built at her expense in Dunkeld;[8] she visited it regularly, supervised the appointment of the teachers and awarded prizes to the scholars. She was interested in agriculture and had a model farm built at Rotmell; she greatly loved the Highlands; and encouraged her cousin-companion Emily MacGregor in the preparation of two volumes on the clan MacGregor.[9]

However, Evelyn's intellectual capabilities and mental stubbornness precluded her from taking the accepted and well-cushioned path of an aristocratic woman. In some ways she seems to have been very like her father in nature. He successfully fulfilled all his many public duties, but an elderly lady in Dunkeld recalled that 'He could not be bothered with high society.'[10] He was happier at home amongst the hills of Atholl and 'the musties' as he affectionately referred to the contents of the Atholl archives when he was compiling the Chronicles of the Atholl and Tullibardine families.[11] This mammoth work, in which he was assisted by Emily MacGregor, took many years to complete.

A handful of upper and middle class women of the period succeeded in indulging their intellectual pursuits. Three examples were the traveller extraordinaire Gertrude Bell,[12] and the twins Agnes and Maggie Smith who became experts in Semetic studies.[13] Accepted as eccentrics, they had advantages over the vast majority of women of that period in that they had financial independence and were not hidebound by the rigid aristocratic rules of acceptable behaviour which trapped Evelyn. Had Evelyn followed her father's example of exercising moderation in pursuit of his personal interests, and maintaining the public role which was expected of him, she would probably have been thought of as merely eccentric. But the obsessive nature of her mental state prevented this. As Weeks and Ward point out, mental illness has long been used 'to account for the diverse kinds of rule-breaking for which society has no better explanation. Eccentrics, on the other hand, are treated more permissively . . . provided they do not threaten too much.'[14] The fact that Evelyn was sent abroad by the Atholl family clearly demonstrates that her mother in particular perceived her as a threat to the established order of an aristocratic household. This affords a revealing insight into the values and priorities in this upper class family at that period, although the exile was intended only as a temporary measure. It was Evelyn herself who chose to make it lifelong.

It is impossible to separate the physical and mental problems which plagued Evelyn throughout her adult life, and yet this woman created two truly unique and wonderful collections. For years only a few specialists in Gaelic folk-lore and fine needlework had heard of Lady Evelyn Stewart Murray, while a handful of Atholl families passed down whispered, half forgotten memories of her when she lived in Perthshire. However, her collection of tales are now being researched with a view to publication in the near future, while her needlework collection in Blair Castle has recently been attracting growing numbers of people from all over the world. It is hoped that this book will reveal to a wider audience the achievements of this outstandingly gifted aristocratic woman who, although she stubbornly refused to keep in step with her class, always remained a true daughter of Atholl.

NOTES

[1] M. Forster, *Significant Sisters: Active Feminism 1839–1939* (1984), 133–165.

[2] L. Tuttle, *Heroines: Women Inspired by Women* (1988), 166.

[3] Forster (1984), 16–52.

[4] *Concise Dictionary of National Biography 1901–1950* (1961), 63–4.

[5] H.M. Jackson, *A Century of Pleasures, Pastimes and Service* (Perth, 1984), 5–6.

[6] J. Manners, Duchess of Rutland, *The Collected Writings of Janetta, Duchess of Rutland* (Edinburgh, 1899).

[7] K. Reynolds, '"A Thorough Gentleman": Class and Gender and the Victorian Aristocratic Woman' (forthcoming D.Phil. thesis, Oxford).

[8] Stewart-Murray, IV (1908), 460.

[9] A.G.M. MacGregor, *History of the Clan MacGregor*, I and II (Edinburgh, 1898 and 1901).

[10] Dunkeld and Birnam Historical Society, *Dunkeld Remembered* (Dundee, 1993), 21.

[11] Stewart-Murray, IV (1908), 520.

[12] J. Keay, *With Passport and Parasol* (1989).

[13] A.W. Price, *The Ladies of Castlebrae* (1985).

[14] D.J. Weeks and K. Ward, *Eccentrics, the Scientific Investigation* (Stirling, 1988), 4.

BIBLIOGRAPHY

UNPUBLISHED SOURCES

Atholl Archives, Bundles 63, 64, 66, 93, l09/2, 421, 423, 425, 429, 458, 470, 480, 482, 484, 487, 489, 491, 492, 501, 508, 519, 526, 527, 528, 529, 530, 634, 647, 930, 945, 955, 981, 996, 1372, 1467, 1472, 1474, 1653, 1657, 1667, KM 82, 83, 83/1, 83/2, 85/2, 163, 166, 480. [Blair Castle]

Education files, ED7/1/80. [Scottish Record Offfice]

Logierait School Log Books (1878 and 1913).

Reynolds, K., '"A Thorough Gentleman": Class and Gender and the Victorian Aristocratic Woman' (forthcoming D.Phil. thesis).

Steinen, K. von den, 'In Search of the Antecedents of Women's Political Activism in Early 18th Century Scotland: The Daughters of Anne, Duchess of Hamilton' (1990).

Victoria, Queen, Unpublished later Journal.

Personal letters: Miss K. Reynolds to S. Robertson; Dr A. Bruford to S. Robertson.

Oral accounts: Mrs Jean Forest to S. Robertson; a number of people who prefer to remain anonymous to S. Robertson.

Malines City Archives, Domiciliary Register.

The Duke of Atholl's Collection.

PUBLISHED SOURCES

Academie Royale des sciences, des lettres and des beaux-arts de Belgique, *Biographie Nationale* (Brussels, 1965).

Bibliothèque Communale de Spa, *La Saison de Spa* (1914).

Blair Collection, SRO.

Bott, A. (ed.), *Our Mothers: Victorian Women 1870–1900* (1932).

Cameron, P., 'Perthshire Gaelic Songs and their Composers', *Transactions of the Gaelic Society of Inverness*, XVII and XVIII (Inverness, 1891 and 1893).

Concise D.N.B., 2 (1961).

Daily Telegraph, 11 December 1936.

Davey, N., *The Tay Bridge Disaster* (Dundee, 1993).

Dunkeld and Birnam Historical Society, *Dunkeld Remembered* (Dundee, 1993).

Fane, S.P., *Memoranda of Procedure at Her Majesty's Drawing Rooms and other Ceremonials* (Privately printed, 1895).

Forster, M., *Significant Sisters: Active Feminism 1839–1939* (1984).

Hamerton, P.G., *Human Intercourse* (1910).

Hamerton, P.G., *The Intellectual Life* (1910).

Hammerton, J. (ed.), *World War 1914–1918* (1919).

Hamilton, E., *Old House at Walton: More about the Mordaunts* (Salisbury, 1988).

Henrey, B., *British Botanical and Horticultural Literature before 1800*, 2 (1975).

Hetherington, S.J., *Against the Tide: Katharine Atholl 1874–1960* (Aberdeen, 1989).

Hunter, J., *The Making of the Crofting Community* (Edinburgh, 1976).

Jackson, H.M., *A Century of Pleasures, Pastimes and Service* (Perth, 1984).

Keay, J., *With Passport and Parasol* (1989).

Loudon, I., 'Chlorosis, Anaemia and Anorexia Nervosa', *British Medical Journal*, 281 (1980).

MacGregor, A.G.M., *History of the Clan MacGregor*, I and II (Edinburgh, 1898 and 1901).

Mallet, V., *Life with Queen Victoria: Marie Mallet's Letters from Court 1887–1901* (1968).

Manners, J., Duchess of Rutland, *The Collected Writings of Janetta, Duchess of Rutland* (Edinburgh, 1899).

Mill, J.S., *The Subjection of Women* (1869).

Morris, B., *Victorian Embroidery* (1962).

Murray, K.M., Duchess of Atholl, *Working Partnership* (1958).

O'Murchu, M., *East Perthshire Gaelic* (Dublin, 1989).

Powell, G.D., *Electricity as used in Rheumatism, Gout and Nervous Affections* (Dublin, 1876).

Price, A.W., *The Ladies of Castlebrae* (1985).

Souhami, D., *A Woman's Place: the Changing Picture of Women in Britain* (1986).

Stewart-Murray, J., 7th Duke of Atholl, *Chronicles of the Atholl and Tullibardine Families*, I and IV (Edinburgh, 1908).

Swain, M., *Historical Needlework – a Study of Influences in Scotland and Northern England* (1970).

Swain, M., *The Flowerers: the Story of Ayrshire White Needlework* (1955).

Trevelyan, G.M., *English Social History* (1967).

Tuttle, L., *Heroines: Women Inspired by Women* (1988).

Victoria, Queen, *Life at the Court of Queen Victoria 1861–1901* (Exeter, 1984).

Wattville, A. de, *A Practical Introduction to Medical Electricity* (1884).

Weeks, D.J. and Ward, K., *Eccentrics, the Scientific Investigation* (Stirling, 1988).